Vancouver Grizzlies

The Official Book

WRITTEN BY DOUG SMITH

Reflecting back on the challenges we faced in bringing one of the world's most exciting games to Vancouver, I can't help but marvel. The exhilaration and pride I felt the day we vaulted over the final hurdle is indescribable. My pride extends to all the staff that made this happen, but especially to Stu Jackson, a man with a heart that could rally a whole city behind the fledgling Grizzlies. Today, we have a young and exciting NBA team led by a fine coach in Brian Winters, and in Orca Bay's General Motors Place, we have one of the sporting world's premier facilities for both players and fans. *Vancouver Grizzlies: The Official Book* takes you through the highlights of bringing you the NBA, the game of basketball and the excitement of its biggest stars.

Co-chairman John McCaw and I believe we're poised on the edge of an incredible time in Vancouver sports history. The Grizzlies are here to play. Watch out Canada!

ARTHUR GRIFFITHS
Co-chairman, Chief Executive Officer and Governor
Vancouver Grizzlies
Orca Bay Sports & Entertainment

A WHITECAP / OPUS BOOK

Island Paper Mills
Luna Gloss Cover 100lb.
Luna Gloss 100lb.

LUNA

Published and produced by Opus Productions Inc.
300 West Hastings Street, Vancouver, British Columbia, Canada V6B 1K6

This edition published in Canada by Whitecap Books Limited, 351 Lynn Avenue, North Vancouver, British Columbia, Canada V7J 2C4
Tel: (604) 980-9852

First Published in 1995

10 9 8 7 6 5 4 3 2 1

Canadian Cataloguing in Publication Data
Smith, Douglas G., 1958-
        Vancouver Grizzlies

        ISBN 1-55110-390-7

        1. Vancouver Grizzlies (Basketball team) I. Title.
GV885.52.V36S64 1995   796.323'64'0971133   C95-911069-0

Printed and bound in Canada
by DW Friesen Ltd.

table of contents

Foreword: *Stu Jackson* 4

Chapter One: *The Franchise* 6

Chapter Two: *The Origins* 18

Chapter Three: *NBA Today* 38

Chapter Four: *The Grizzlies* 90

Grizzlies Player Profiles 108

Grizzlies 1995-96 Schedule 110

Acknowledgements 111

Since I first joined the Vancouver Grizzlies organization and moved to British Columbia during the summer of 1994, I've been counting the days leading up to the debut of the National Basketball Association in Canada.

From the beginning, I've sensed the excitement building and marvelled at how our new franchise has been embraced by people from all walks of life, throughout B.C. and across Canada. We've worked hard to respond to this excitement with an approach to building our team based on community involvement. Our commitment is reflected in the partnerships we've established, including those with Basketball B.C., the B.C. High School Boys Basketball Association, the B.C. Secondary School Girls Basketball Association and B.C.'s Maple Leaf Wheelchair Basketball Association, along with Basketball Canada. These community partnerships will combine with corporate partnerships to facilitate a series of quality programs for our next generation of Canadian young people.

I'm very proud of the dedicated organization we've drawn together to the cause of promoting and growing NBA basketball in particular and basketball in general.

Together, all of us associated with the Vancouver Grizzlies face great challenges and even greater opportunities. There's a sense of history linked with almost everything we're doing in laying the groundwork for our franchise and our fans. That's been very exciting for all of us, from our owners, Arthur R. Griffiths and John E. McCaw, Jr., to the part-time event staff that will work our games at brand new General Motors Place in downtown Vancouver.

It's all coming together in a country that might be new to the NBA, but thanks to the Canadian inventor of the game, Dr. James A. Naismith, is certainly not new to basketball.

The sport itself has become the number one high school sport in Canada. We know that Canadians' love for hockey has typically been passed down from their parents. Canada's love for NBA basketball will for the most part work the other way and will rely on the passion for the game being passed along from young people to adults, from children to their parents.

This book is a testimonial to this strong tradition. It's a tribute to the birth and development of the Vancouver Grizzlies and our Canadian NBA expansion cousins, the Toronto Raptors. It's a reflection of the colour and excitement of the NBA. Moreover, it speaks to the great potential for basketball in Canada.

Our new fans will be the ultimate judges of our success on and off the court. We'll work hard to do the things necessary to make more Canadians aware of the special magic of the NBA, the talent and athleticism of our players, the excitement of our game, the entertainment and sheer accessibility of basketball for people of all ages.

Therein lies the responsibility we carry for the NBA and the game of basketball in Canada.

STU JACKSON
*Executive Vice President of Basketball Operations
and General Manager
Vancouver Grizzlies
Orca Bay Sports & Entertainment*

NATIONAL BASKETBALL ASSOCIATION

OLYMPIC TOWER · 645 FIFTH AVENUE · NEW YORK, N.Y. 10022 · 212-826-7000

May 15, 1995

Vancouver Basketball Limited Partnership
780 Beatty Street, Third Floor
Vancouver, British Columbia
V6B 2M1

Re: Expansion Agreement dated April 27, 1994, as amended, between the 27 Entities that then constituted the National Basketball Association (the "Grantors") and Vancouver Basketball Limited Partnership (the "Expansion Agreement")

Dear Sir:

In my capacity as Commissioner of the National Basketball Association (the "NBA"), I am writing to advise you that the NBA has received the aggregate consideration required to be delivered pursuant to, and the closing documents under, the Expansion Agreement. Consequently, the Franchise (as defined in the Expansion Agreement), has been duly granted to Vancouver Basketball Limited Partnership in accordance with the Expansion Agreement and the Constitution and By-Laws of the NBA, subject to the rights of the Grantors and the NBA set forth therein and in the closing documents.

Congratulations and welcome to the NBA.

Very truly yours,

David J. Stern

cc: Arthur R. Griffiths, Chairman and Governor
John E. McCaw, Jr., Vice-Chairman
Michael J. Korenberg, Deputy Chairman
Stanley B. McCammon, Executive Vice-President
John H. Chapple, President
Tod Leiweke, Executive Vice-President, Business
Stuart W. Jackson, Vice-President, Basketball Operations
& General Manager
David G. Cobb, Vice-President, Finance

a b o v e : *It's official! Letter from Commissioner David J. Stern*
awarding an NBA franchise to Vancouver's Griffiths-McCaw group.

The thought of an NBA franchise first came to Arthur Griffiths when a Toronto group caught the attention of the

FRANCHISE

league's expansion committee in 1993. Conceding that Toronto would probably be the chosen city if the NBA awarded just one new team to an international interest, Griffiths knew Vancouver would be a logical and natural second addition.

And that possibility was too good not to pursue. While Griffiths had some expertise in franchise expansion from his ownership of the Canucks, nothing he had seen before prepared him for what lay ahead.

"As it turns out, the process was quite a bit different," he recalls. "In hockey, when we expanded, we would send out an expansion agreement and say, if you sign and do the following things, this is what it will cost and this is how you pay and this is what you need to do.

"In basketball, we sort of found out along the way, after we said we were interested, what it would cost and, more important, how we were supposed to accomplish certain objectives and when they were to be done by. I had a lot of great support from the expansion committee and it was a great comfort to be welcomed the way we were."

Arthur Griffiths made his first foray into the world of professional sports at the age of 23, working in the Vancouver Canucks' ticket office for his well-respected father, the hockey team's owner, Frank Griffiths, Sr. Few believed Griffiths would remain behind the scenes for very long, but fewer still could

have predicted this would turn into such an extraordinary story. It is the tale of a young man who has become a leader in his community, and has strived to give his city a strong and lasting legacy in the world of sports and entertainment.

Griffiths realized what was important to any project's success early in his life after a failed tryout for the rugby team at Vancouver's St. George's school. It wasn't just the stars, it was the sum of the parts, and he was willing to play a role as the team's manager. "One thing school taught me was to work with people and be a member of a team."

It is that spirit of teamwork that has allowed Griffiths to survive in the ultra-competitive world of professional sports. Elevated in 1981 to Assistant to the Chairman of the Canucks – the rather formidable personage of his father – and then assuming daily control of the venture six years later, Griffiths has surrounded and aligned himself with talented people with solid skills, and together they have seen his enterprises flourish.

Before Frank Griffiths, Sr. passed away in 1994, it became apparent that for the family's first sporting venture – the Vancouver Canucks – to continue to thrive, the team would

facing page: *The Grizzlies and their neighbours, perennial league leaders the Seattle SuperSonics, in future will contend for the right to boast they're the best on the Northwest Coast.* left: *Griffiths family friend John E. McCaw, Jr. (right) helped fuel the Vancouver bid.*

need a new home. But that home, which was to ultimately become the gorgeous, privately financed General Motors Place, needed another complementary enterprise to add to the foundation already laid by the hockey team. The logical choice was NBA basketball, on the cutting edge of professional sports and skyrocketing in popularity. An opportunity arose for Vancouver to pounce when the league decided to expand to Canada. Toronto would get one franchise, Vancouver the other, and Arthur Griffiths would lead that western charge.

The decision to add a second Canadian franchise was not a difficult one for the NBA to make. The league governors were impressed with all facets of the operation, from the arena, which was already under construction, to the dynamics of the city. A natural rival for Seattle and Portland in the Pacific Northwest and as a gateway to the market of the Pacific Rim, Vancouver was an ideal extension of the league's growth plans.

League governors, who were at one time content just to add one team, saw the potential in Vancouver and the solid leadership of Griffiths. Once the group started to state its case, adding a second Canadian team was almost a foregone conclusion.

"Our last expansion taught us that a league can get a supercharge from expansion to exciting places," Commissioner David Stern said as the decision was about to be made to add Vancouver. "We're thrilled to welcome Vancouver into the NBA. The Griffiths family has been a model of professional sports ownership for many, many years."

To help his arena thrive, and to help his city become an even greater player in the North American sports world, Griffiths needed some help. Due to the massive financial load — $163 million Cdn. for the arena, $125 million U.S. in NBA expansion fees — Griffiths ultimately brought in long-time family friend John E. McCaw, Jr. of Seattle, whose involvement as financial partner would allow Griffiths to achieve his goal of bringing together the NHL, the NBA and a world-class arena.

"It wasn't possible to do the things we wanted to do, without a change. The way I looked at this process — and there were so many different dynamics, whether it was the Grizzlies or the arena and, of course, the Canucks — what was really important was that whatever we did here was bigger than just the ownership issue. It had to embody our culture."

left: *Throwing their hat in the ring: The Grizzlies logo embodies the power and ferocity of one of nature's proudest creatures. The team's stylish merchandise vaulted to the upper levels of NBA sales.*

The synergy between McCaw, the former co-owner of the giant McCaw Cellular Communications firm, and Griffiths will allow the Grizzlies to prosper as the newest sporting venture in Vancouver. The new controlling company – Orca Bay Sports & Entertainment – promises to offer the best in sports and entertainment in Canada, with the Grizzlies, Canucks and General Motors Place ready to satisfy the demands of any sports fan. And it is Griffiths, whose family has a long and illustrious history of owning and fostering sports and entertainment properties in Vancouver, who is at the helm as Co-chairman and Chief Executive Officer.

But before the team could ever set foot on the floor there was plenty of work to do and many goals to be accomplished – it was a process that began even before the franchise had been awarded. The first thing Griffiths had to do was find a strong visual identity in order to launch the bid for the franchise. The "Vancouver Mounties" had the instantly recognizable name and image that he wanted in a team entity. However, "Mounties" was not to be. In the world of NBA marketing, the biggest necessity of a new entity is clear title worldwide, and "Mounties," it so happened, were everywhere, from other professional sports teams to souvenir stands all around the globe. There was no way the team could get copyrights on the name everywhere they were necessary, so the team name had to be changed.

Enter "Grizzlies," in what proved to be a perfect fit. The animal indigenous to the Pacific Northwest and with roots deep in native culture was a logical choice for the team. The bear's traits – strength, agility, power and spirit – are the kinds of traits Griffiths wants his team to display.

There can be no minimizing the importance of developing a new franchise's name and logo. Everything about the team – from the uniforms its players wear to an endless assortment of clothing and merchandise – will bear the colours (Pacific Turquoise, Naismith Red, Bear Bronze and black) and the logo that spring from the name. When the change was made, "Grizzlies" came naturally, and the name has worked well in the developmental process, since the new team's merchandise has quickly jumped into the top 10 in worldwide sale of NBA products.

There were other, equally important tasks to complete. The most pressing was the NBA's demands that deposits be in hand for 12,500 season-tickets before the end of 1994 – no small task for any franchise, expansion or otherwise.

Superstar City: In Orca Bay's General Motors Place, Vancouver now possesses a worthy venue to welcome the greats. top: *Local hero Bryan Adams added his international stature to the stadium's sold-out opening night concert, September 19, 1995.* bottom: *Vancouver Canucks season opener vs. Detroit Red Wings, October 9, 1995, brings hockey downtown.*

above: *In hardworking Stu Jackson, the Grizzlies have their basketball Renaissance man. Jackson's background in the sport marks him as a true leader, and his integrity has helped the team win over Vancouver fans and media.*

So the full-court press began, an educational process for sports fans in Vancouver who may not have had the fullest knowledge of NBA basketball, and a selling process for those who did. A concerted advertising campaign, and a clear demonstration that the goal was one that had to be met or the team would never see the light of day, resulted in success for Griffiths and the management team he had put together. Executive Vice President of Business Tod Leiweke was brought in from the Golden State Warriors, and his work during the elongated season-ticket drive helped the Grizzlies meet what was one of the most difficult challenges laid down by the NBA.

"I think there have been a lot of closet fans – that's the best way I can describe it – and that's who we were able to reach," said Griffiths. "There have been people who have played the game and watched the game and now they can be part of the NBA experience. It's important for the Grizzlies to be part of the fabric of our community. It took a lot of time and a tremendous commitment to expose the Grizzlies in the community and I think we accomplished that."

The drive, as big a civic event as any in the city's sports history, got a huge boost from none other than retired NBA star Magic Johnson. The 11-time All-Star and former Dream Teamer travelled up the coast from his home in Los Angeles in December 1994 to press the flesh and preach the gospel of the NBA.

Griffiths recalls of those hectic months: "There was a great sense of excitement, when you have a ticket drive and the funding of the purchase of the team and the selection of a manager and the name and all of those issues. There was a lot going on. But we managed to draw upon some fantastic people in every aspect of this business to make the things happen in a first-class manner. What we've got as an organization is a great sense of family – that's very important to us."

To lead the family, Griffiths looked to a man with skills at every level of basketball and its administration. Stu Jackson, a former NBA coach, NBA front office executive, college coach and highly respected basketball man, signed on as Vice President and General Manager in July 1994 in the biggest hiring Griffiths had to make.

right: *A visit from much-beloved NBA legend Magic Johnson gave Vancouver's season-ticket drive a timely boost. "It's going to be entertainment for a night that you can't get anywhere else," Johnson said during his Vancouver appearance. "The team is like a new baby being born. Take it. Embrace it. Love it. Nurture it. See it through as it grows up."*
far right: *To debut their new team uniform, Grizzlies imported supermodel and former volleyball star Gabrielle Reece, here seen joking with Arthur Griffiths at the Grizzlies' fashion show.*

A former head coach of the New York Knicks, Jackson is under no illusions as he takes his new position. He has been part of every aspect of the franchise's development, from the season-ticket drive to the naming process to the corporate sponsorships to the expansion and college drafts, and he knows the team will always be a work in progress.

"The challenge is enormous and it's not a process that is going to start and complete itself overnight," Jackson said when he took the job. "I'm just a young man who really enjoys the challenge of this and the work that is involved. That is what motivates me."

Jackson has not had to make his journey alone, since Griffiths has populated the Grizzlies' front office with talented, aggressive people in every area of the operation. An endeavour as grand as a professional sports franchise requires total dedication from everyone involved, from the senior managers down to the junior staffers in every department, from business to basketball.

And, of course, the basketball side of things is in good hands. Brian Winters, who served as an assistant coach with the Atlanta Hawks under veteran coach Lenny Wilkens, was named the team's first head coach. Director of Scouting Larry Riley, one of the most respected judges of talent in the league, signed on after working for the Milwaukee Bucks. The combination of Winters' skills in teaching the game and Riley's skills in discovering new talent demonstrate the dedication Griffiths and Jackson have to putting together a first-class basketball operation.

The Vancouver Grizzlies basketball team is the realization of a dream. Along with John McCaw, Arthur Griffiths has invited others to share in this dream, to share the rewards as well as the enormous responsibility that goes with running an NBA team, an NHL team and a brand new, multi-purpose facility. He takes great pride in what he and those around him have already accomplished, and what can be accomplished in the future, as the long-standing tradition of sports excellence in Vancouver continues. In joining the ranks of the NBA, he links his own family's accomplishments with another great tradition, which stems from a dream nurtured by another public-spirited Canadian, just a storied and colourful century ago.

far left: *Director of Scouting Larry Riley shown with the first player ever signed by a Canadian NBA team, free agent Kevin Pritchard.*
left: *Head Coach Brian Winters brings a winning tradition to Vancouver from his years spent as an assistant coach under Lenny Wilkens, who holds the NBA record for career coaching victories.*
facing page: *The NBA's best will be thrilling Canadian fans, and pictured here are two of the league's most brilliant luminaries: Michael Jordan and Shaquille O'Neal.*

T H E

above: *Abundant harvest: From humble beginnings, the sport of basketball has grown to world stature. Peach baskets served as goals for the first game.*
facing page: *Dr. James A. Naismith, 1861-1939, the inventor of the game.*

A goalkeeper, two guards, three centre men and two wings took their places

O R I G I N S

on the hardwood floor at the Young Men's Christian Association gymnasium in Springfield, Massachusetts, on a December day in 1891, facing a like number of contemporaries deployed on the other side of the gym's centre line.

top: *Naismith (second row, right) with his original team, December 1891.* **bottom:** *Organized professional contests were held within two or three years of that first game in Springfield, and the National League, the first in a revolving-door series of early pro leagues, was formed in 1898. The Buffalo Germans (pictured) dominated their competition, amassing a 792-86 record – including an 111-game winning streak – between 1895 and 1929.*

Basketball's birthplace: The YMCA Training School gymnasium Springfield, Massachusetts, circa 1891.

Dressed in long-sleeved jerseys and long grey trousers, they were about to indulge their instructor in his attempt to devise some type of recreational activity for the winter months that didn't involve the rough-house tactics of rugby or lacrosse, two sports the instructor knew intimately, but two he also realized didn't translate well to the indoor forum.

Around the room was suspended a balcony for spectators that also doubled as a running track for men trying to keep up their physical fitness. It was a dimly lit gym, about 45 feet wide and 65 feet long. The playing surface, marked out not with painted lines but with clubs, dumbbells and the other trappings of a gymnastics class of the era, measured somewhere in the neighbourhood of 35 by 50 feet.

Suspended from the balconies at either end, thanks to the quick thinking of "Pop" Stebbins, the YMCA's janitor known for his packrat tendencies, were two peach baskets, their 15-inch diameter openings tapered to about eight inches at the bottom. The ball was an Association football, the type used for many other games and chosen for this new endeavour simply by

chance. The seemingly simple object of the game was to get the ball into the opponents' basket.

With Stebbins standing by with a step-ladder to retrieve balls that might nestle in the bottom of the peach baskets – only later were the bottoms cut out – the boys played for about 45 minutes, managing just once to get the ball in the basket. Nevertheless, that goal by William R. Chase from near the mid-point line (the first three-pointer?) set the wheels in motion.

The sporting spectrum would be forever changed from that December day forward, and the young instructor felt a sense of accomplishment when the class ended. It took a while for his newfangled game to gain universal acceptance, and the predictable growing pains at times made it appear as if it would not survive. But with that one toss of the ball, the one basket by William R. Chase and the decision to offer young men an alternative to the games they had known, the young YMCA instructor by the name of James A. Naismith had invented basketball. Little did he know, the game would turn into one of the most popular sports worldwide.

In the gently rolling hills of eastern Ontario lies the tiny town of Almonte, population about 4,400, and with the same look as countless other rural communities in countless other provinces and states.

From this sleepy Ontario town, James A. Naismith began an incredible life's journey that took him to Montreal, to Springfield, to Denver and to Kansas. Orphaned as a youngster when his parents died of typhoid, young Naismith moved to Almonte where he lived with an aunt and uncle. As a teen, he decided to dedicate his life to the ministry and enrolled in the Presbyterian College of McGill University in Montreal. As with many struggling young students, he had to find a way to make the money to pay for his education, so he took a job as a physical education instructor at a nearby gymnasium. Naismith saw a correlation between spiritual and physical fitness and enrolled in the School for Christian Workers in Springfield after his graduation from divinity school.

That School for Christian Workers soon became the Young Men's Christian Association Training School, and it was there that Naismith, a 30-year-old temporary instructor of physical education, held that historic first game of basketball. While he initially developed the game as one of a more genteel nature than rugby or lacrosse, the bumps and bruises he saw set him on another path – to medical school in Denver where he added an MD degree to his rapidly growing list of accomplishments. Naismith finally settled at the University of Kansas, where he taught and helped refine such sports as fencing, golf, track, rowing and lacrosse. He served as the school's director of physical education until he was replaced by the legendary Forrest "Phog" Allen in the mid-1920s.

As one would expect from a divinity school graduate, YMCA instructor and college professor, Naismith was an altruistic sort who saw athletics in their purest and most simple of terms, keeping young men healthy of body and healthy of mind. But natural selection dictated that basketball would not remain a game played in tiny gyms in out-of-the-way locations. Basketball would evolve, and it was only a matter of time before it joined the ranks of the professional sporting world.

left: *In the countryside near Ottawa, on the outskirts of the quiet town of Almonte, sits an historic landmark plaque commemorating Naismith's childhood home. Inside the house, now a museum, memorabilia tells the story of the father of basketball and the origins of the game.*
facing page: *James A. Naismith lived to see the game he invented flourish to national popular appeal. Naismith is pictured here at the University of Kansas, where he was director of physical education.*

Circa 1910 basketball that was found above
Naismith's office at the University of Kansas.

ORIGINAL RULES

The NBA rule book is a complex and sometimes confusing piece of legislation, governing such happenstance as shattered backboards, 24-second clocks, illegal defences, fights between players, uniform numbers and the colour of shoes.

James Naismith's first set of rules, set down in December 1891, were simple and to the point:

The ball is to be an ordinary Association foot ball.

1. The ball may be thrown in any direction with one or both hands.

2. The ball may be batted in any direction with one or both hands (never with the fist).

3. A player cannot run with the ball; the player must throw it from the spot on which he catches it; allowance to be made for a man who catches the ball when running at a good speed.

4. The ball must be held in or between the hands; the arms or body must not be used for holding it.

5. No shouldering, holding, pushing, tripping or striking in any way the person of an opponent shall count as a foul. The first infringement of this rule by any person shall count as a foul, the second shall disqualify him until the next goal is made, or if there was evident intent to injure the person, for the whole of the game, no substitution allowed.

6. A foul is striking at the ball with the fist, violation of Rules 3 and 4, and such as described in Rule 5.

7. If either side makes three consecutive fouls, it shall count as a goal for the opponents (consecutive means without the opponents in the meantime making a foul).

8. A goal shall be made when the ball is thrown or batted from the ground into the basket and stays there, providing those defending the goal do not touch or disturb the goal. If the ball rests on the edge and the opponent moves the basket, it shall count as a goal.

9. When the ball goes out of bounds it shall be thrown into the field and played by the person first touching it. In case of a dispute the umpire shall throw it straight into the field. The thrower in is allowed five seconds; if he holds it longer it shall go to the opponent. If any side persists in delaying the game, the umpire shall call a foul on them.

10. The umpire shall be judge of the men, and shall note the fouls, and notify the referee when three consecutive fouls have been made. He shall have the power to disqualify men according to Rule 5.

11. The referee shall be judge of the ball and shall decide when the ball is in play, in bounds, and to which side it belongs, and shall keep the time. He shall decide when a goal has been made, and keep account of the goals with any other duties that are usually performed by a referee.

12. The time shall be two fifteen minute halves, with five minutes rest between.

13. The side making the most goals in that time shall be declared winners. In case of a draw the game may, by agreement of the captains, be continued until another goal is made.

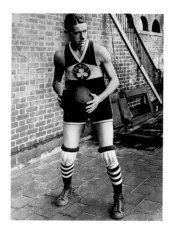

Franchises came and went, affiliations changed, so the best teams switched to barnstorming the cities of the East and the Midwest, playing challenge matches against local heroes. In the rough and tumble epoch between the wars, one team personified finesse: New York City's Original Celtics. Nat Holman (pictured), renowned for his passing ability and deceptive ball-handling manoeuvres, was a Celtic standout.

November 1, 1946, Toronto, Ontario, Maple Leaf Gardens: That night the crowds milled about outside, waiting to become part of history. The venerable hockey shrine, open for about 15 years, was going to play host to the first-ever game of the Basketball Association of America, pitting the Toronto Huskies against the New York Knickerbockers, and there was excitement in the air.

Basketball had come a long way since that day in Springfield. Barnstorming teams had criss-crossed the United States spreading the gospel. The college game had taken off; Madison Square Garden in New York was the mecca of the game, playing host to college doubleheaders that were the envy of basketball promoters everywhere. Still, the game was thought of as a college game. The professional leagues that sprung up regionally in the northeast and midwest of the country had not caught on.

But with the Second World War ending, tens of thousands of young men and women would need something to fill their leisure hours, and the owners of ice arenas and professional hockey teams needed something to help fill the seats and vacant dates. Thus was born the Basketball Association of America, led by the president of the American Hockey League, Maurice Podoloff, and tied tightly to the homes of hockey teams in cities such as Toronto, Pittsburgh, Cleveland, Boston and New York. Podoloff, a Canadian citizen, was the fledgling league's first president and later became the NBA's inaugural president.

In Toronto, curiosity ruled the day. Charles Watson, an official with Canadian Breweries Ltd., was the president of the team and had convinced industrialist H. S. Shannon, local stockbroker Eric Cradock and Ben Newman, a businessman from St. Catharines, Ontario, to take a chance on the new league. Realizing the game itself might be a tough sell, Watson persuaded one of the best known sports figures of the era, Lew Hayman, to come on board as general manager.

So all eyes were on the Gardens that evening. The game attracted 7,090 fans to the shrine of hockey who sat excitedly through the game New York eventually won 68-66. It was the beginning of what the Toronto owners hoped was a long association with the new league. This was not to be.

Ed Sadowski, signed away from Fort Wayne, Indiana, to a lucrative $10,000 contract to be the player/coach of the Huskies, quickly found out he wasn't cut out for both duties.

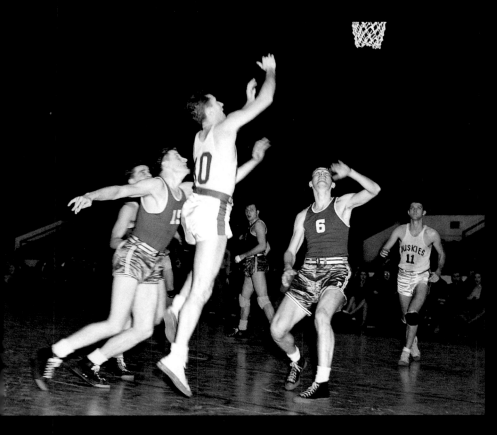

top: *The Basketball Association of America was the precursor to the NBA: Here, the Toronto Huskies and Pittsburgh Ironmen play at Maple Leaf Gardens in December 1946.* **bottom:** *Huskies' Dick Fitzgerald, left, and Clarence "Kleggie" Hermsen take a breather alongside coach Bob "Red" Rolfe.*

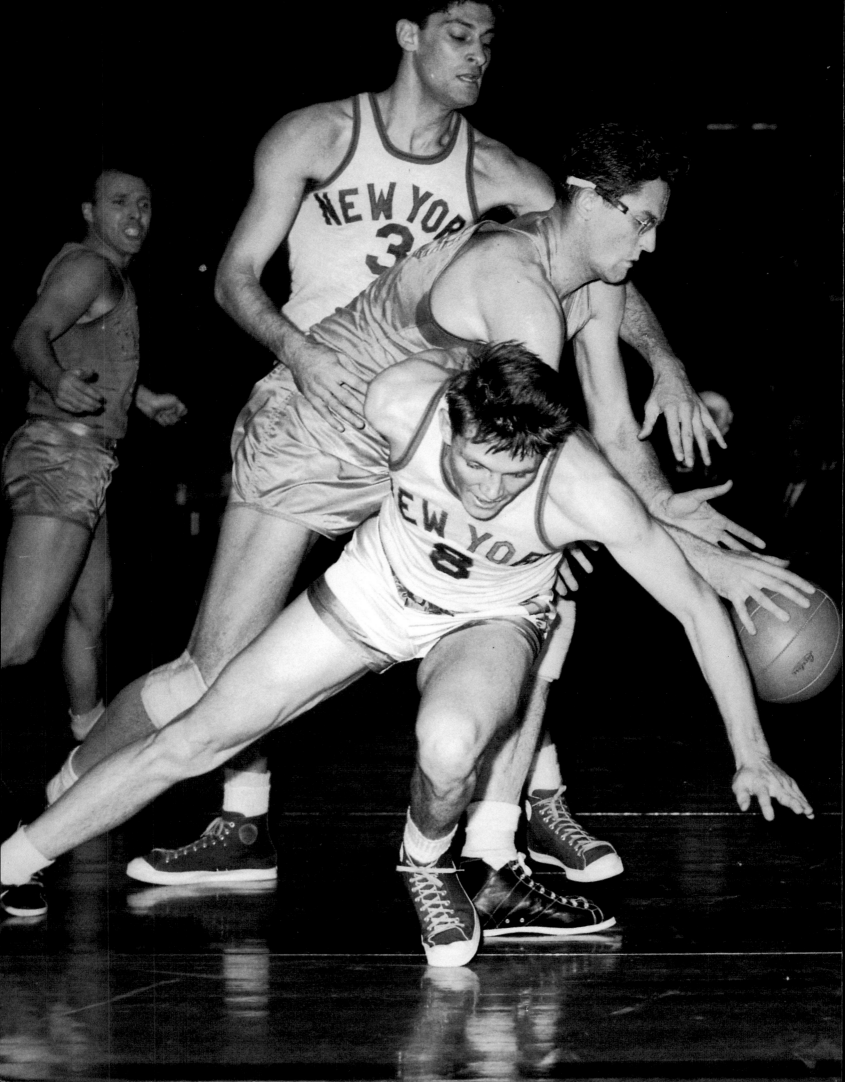

The team got off to a 3-8 start – hardly the way to attract new fans to a winter sport in the home of the Toronto Maple Leafs. Hayman had little choice but to try to persuade his high-priced athlete to give up his coaching duties and concentrate solely on playing, but Sadowski bolted from the team during a road trip to Providence, and the Huskies were sinking like a stone.

Hayman filled in as coach for one game – a loss – before turning over the helm to "Red" Rolfe, a starter with baseball's New York Yankees and a former basketball coach at Yale University. The Huskies continued to limp along, struggling home with a miserable 22-38 record, tied for dead last in the league's Eastern Division with the Boston Celtics. Attendance plummeted, the financial losses mounted, and the Basketball Association of America experiment north of the 49th parallel came to an end in June of 1947 when Hayman pulled the plug.

The growing pains of any new venture are harsh; those of a new professional sports league are that much harsher. After the first eventful season – Philadelphia beat Chicago four games to one to win the inaugural championship – the Basketball Association of America franchises in Toronto, Cleveland, Pittsburgh and Detroit folded. By the time the 1949-50 season rolled around, the BAA had expanded and contracted, grown and shrunk and finally absorbed six franchises from the rival, Midwest-based National Basketball League. Wanting to come up with a fresh new look, name and image, the National Basketball Association was born.

There were 17 teams in the new league, from New York to Sheboygan, Denver to Washington, Boston to Minneapolis. George Mikan, the most talked about basketball player on earth at the time, a six-foot-10 giant who would revolutionize the game, was the league's marquee player. In what would become known as the Mikan Era, he led the Minneapolis Lakers to five championships between 1949 and 1954 and was literally and figuratively a towering figure in the world of sports. A brilliant player at Chicago's DePaul University, Mikan was able to bring to the NBA many of the fans who watched him throughout his college career, and he went on to be voted Mr. Basketball of the First Half Century for his play in college and in the pros. He was the first player to become synonymous with the league, but he certainly wasn't the last.

facing page: *Dominant BAA star George Mikan drives between two Knicks defenders during a 1948 game.*
right: *Mikan and fellow Minnesota Lakers visit the White House while in town for the final BAA championship series in 1949.*
far right: *Over a nine-year professional career Mikan averaged 21.5 points per game and 13.4 rebounds per game.*

far left: *Bob Cousy (left) starred for more than a decade with the Boston Celtics' dynasty of the 1950s and 1960s. High-scoring Elgin Baylor brought greatness to the Lakers during the same era.*
left: *Future Hall-of-Famers Jerry West (left) and Oscar Robertson pose before the 1960 NCAA All-Star Game.*
facing page: *Bill Russell and Wilt Chamberlain locked horns throughout the 1960s and re-wrote the job description for NBA big men: Chamberlain on offence, Russell for the defence. Together they won nine MVPs (four for Chamberlain and five for Russell).*

There have been dynasties in every sport and every sporting era. The New York Yankees treated baseball's World Series like their own rite of autumn in the 1950s and 1960s; the Montreal Canadiens were perennial Stanley Cup champions in the same era. But few teams in any sport in any league in any country in the world can match the success of the Boston Celtics of the NBA. Playing in the magical and mystical Boston Garden – where leprechauns lived and general manager Red Auerbach made sure the opposition was treated with predictable hostility and cold water in the locker room – the Celtics of the Bill Russell era were unmatched in their success.

In 1956-57, in every season between 1958-59 and 1965-66 and again in 1967-68 and 1968-69, the Celtics were NBA champions. Russell, the six-foot-10 centre from the University of San Francisco, and Bob Cousy, the magician of the backcourt from Holy Cross, were the league's dominant duo. Cousy led the NBA in assists for eight straight seasons. Russell was the anchor of the frontcourt and was also the single greatest defender of his time, a brilliant shot-blocker who corralled 21,721 rebounds in his career. He won 11 NBA titles in 13 seasons, was the

league's Most Valuable Player five times and appeared in 12 All-Star Games. For many fans, Russell and Cousy and the Celtics *were* the NBA.

Russell's perfect foil was his most bitter rival, Wilt Chamberlain. Where Russell was the dominant defender and a perennial member of a championship team, Chamberlain was the most gifted offensive performer of his era. Although he amassed 31,419 points in a 14-year career, Chamberlain won but two NBA titles: 1967 with the Philadelphia 76ers and 1972 with the Los Angeles Lakers. His teams lost to Russell and the Celtics in three other championship series.

There can be no denying Chamberlain's offensive prowess. On the night of March 2, 1962, playing for the Philadelphia Warriors against the New York Knickerbockers, the big man scored 100 points – an NBA record which has yet to be seriously challenged. He was 36 of 63 from the field, 28 of 32 from the free-throw line. That night, he scored 23 points in the first quarter, 18 in the second, 28 in the third and ended the incredible evening with a 31-point fourth quarter – the single greatest offensive output in NBA history.

To fully appreciate where the league is, it's wise to consider where it once was. There was a time in the not-too-distant past when the NBA didn't enjoy nearly the kind of fame, fortune and adulation it has today and was in danger of disappearing. In the early and mid-1970s, it was a league on the decline. Attendance was down, allegations of drug use by some players had created a negative public image, and there were serious concerns about the league's future. Television networks all but ignored the game as the league's championship series wasn't deemed popular or important enough to rate live network coverage.

But as the 1970s became the 1980s, those difficulties were solved. The drug problem was eradicated by a combination of enlightened leadership in the players union and forward-thinking, aggressive campaigns from the league office. The technological advances in telecommunications, so critical to today's game, came fast and furious, and the league's fortunes were altered permanently. It was like magic.

Or, rather, it was Magic.

To understand why the NBA is where it is today, why the 1990s have been so good, one has to look to the 1980s. And that examination has to start with the brilliant smile and gifted athleticism of Earvin "Magic" Johnson. More than any player in contemporary time, Johnson gave the NBA life. He redefined the playing of the game, doing in a six-foot-nine-inch frame what used to be the sole domain of the little man. He dribbled the ball with that grin lighting up arenas, he threw those picture-perfect no-look passes – always, it seemed, staring into a television camera when he flipped the ball over his shoulder. As a rookie in 1979-80, he took the Los Angeles Lakers to the NBA title, playing centre in the final game for the injured Kareem Abdul-Jabbar. His joy was palpable, his enthusiasm contagious, and he became synonymous with the fun that the NBA has now become.

Four more times in that decade – in 1982, 1985, 1987 and 1988 – he took his team to the top of the mountain. He helped make Lakers games "Showtime" for the Hollywood entertainment jetset. And, if the movie stars liked it and sat in the front rows for the games, it was only a matter of time before the general public took notice.

far left: *Magic Johnson shares a lighter moment with teammates on the bench.*
left: *With his stellar play and sparkling personality, Magic captivated fans throughout the 1980s, and inspired his Lakers to four NBA Championships.*
facing page: *Simply Magic: Throughout the 1980s, one player's name was synonymous with basketball for much of the world. Earvin "Magic" Johnson redefined the game as it is played from the guard position. Along the way, he inspired and delighted a new generation of NBA fans.*

But Johnson needed a rival who was his equal to bring out his very best. While he was working his magic in the make-believe world of Hollywood, his alter-ego was doing the same across the continent in Boston, where Larry Bird, the quiet young man from French Lick, Indiana, was enhancing the already-rich Celtic tradition. Johnson was gregarious, Bird more understated. Johnson was flashy, Bird workmanlike. Each man brought greatness to his team. Bird's team won NBA Championships in 1981, 1984 and 1986. Three times Bird and Johnson met in the NBA Finals. Twice the Lakers were victorious and once the Celtics ruled on the day.

The two men, so different in mannerism but so similar in skill, dedication and determination, were the perfect bookends to help establish the league. Johnson and Bird demonstrated that there were places in the pantheon of greats for men who played different styles of the game in contemporary times.

Johnson played at breakneck speed, getting out fast on the break, pounding the ball up the court at every opportunity. He was a giant among guards and teams were in a quandary about how to stop him. He was too tall for the normal guard to handle; he controlled the ball too well for a forward to defend. He showed fans, coaches and opponents that big men need not wait for the ball to come to them. He invented the big guard position, perfected it, and set the standard by which all others are measured.

At the other end of the court was Bird, not blessed with the natural athletic brilliance of Johnson, but no less a complete player. He had an uncanny knack for getting open for his patent jump shot, and he worked tirelessly every minute he was on the floor. Where Johnson changed the game, Bird showed there was still a place for guile and hard work as much as there was a place for speed and leaping ability.

As chroniclers of the game delve into the contributions of Julius Erving, Magic Johnson, Larry Bird, Isiah Thomas, Michael Jordan, Shaquille O'Neal, Hakeem Olajuwon and the rest of the more contemporary superstars, they cannot overlook the likes of George Mikan, Bob Cousy, Bill Russell, Wilt Chamberlain, Elgin Baylor, Oscar Robertson and Jerry West and the roles they played in bringing the game to prominence in the sporting universe.

a b o v e : *Sphere of influence: Today's fine-tuned Official NBA Basketball bears little resemblance to Naismith's original Association football.*

f a c i n g p a g e : *Three-peat? Hoping to carry last season's glory into the next, 1995 Playoff MVP Hakeem Olajuwon, draped in Houston Rockets' new uniform, cradles his trophy.*

In a bygone era an aura of polite attentiveness carried the sporting day in arenas and stadiums throughout

T O D A Y

North America. There were no raucous antics, no celebrities in the front rows. Overwhelming importance was placed on the sport, and entertainment was left to the movie houses and theatres. That was then. And this is now.

far left: *Fans in Houston cheer on their Rockets during the 1995 NBA Finals.*
left: *Mexico City gets into the NBA spirit during an exhibition game. The NBA also plays exhibition games in Japan and Europe, taking its excitement to an international audience.*

The house lights dim as the performers prepare to take their places on the stage. The spotlights shine with white hot intensity and laser lights dance across the floor. The music – pulsating, modern, loud music – thunders out of dozens of mammoth speakers, exhorting the audience into a frenzy. At every break in the action, something happens. An acrobatic team here, a dance team there, a mascot playing to the crowd. A cornucopia of sights and sounds makes every night in the NBA a memorable one.

Welcome to the NBA, where sports and entertainment are linked at every level, and every game's a festival.

"Our teams have recognized a phenomenon of the 1990s – that fans want very much to be part of the experience," says NBA Commissioner David Stern. "They have really focused on the entire entertainment experience."

And no one does it better than the NBA.

In the contemporary world of professional sports leagues, the NBA has become the benchmark by which all others are measured. It has taken the entire sports industry to new levels. Its influence reaches far beyond the borders of its member cities and into nearly every country on the globe. Its era of growth has made basketball unquestionably The Game of the 1990s. The many reasons for its extraordinary success are varied and diverse.

"In our case, the owners and the teams and the league office and the television networks began work on a lot of different fronts, and they all seemed to come together," is how the commissioner explains the steady growth. "The boom in arenas, the boom in cable television and network television, the boom in sports league-identified merchandise, the boom in TV outside of the United States, the boom in technology through direct satellite broadcasts, CD-ROM, interactivity, the Internet. The growth in all those areas has been tremendously important in contributing to our growth."

Added to this is the attractiveness of the sport and its players. In the simplest of terms, basketball – NBA basketball – is the perfect game for its time. The court, 94 by 50 feet, is a perfect fit for television and allows the kind of closeups that give even the fan at home a sense of being involved in the action. The intensity of the action can be seen in the eyes of the players, up close and personal, which lends an intimacy to the game that exists in no other sport.

The dance teams in action. **top:** *Houston's Rocket Power Dancers and Turbo, the team mascot.* **bottom, left:** *One of Chicago's Luva Bulls.* **bottom, right:** *A member of the Denver Nuggets Performance Dance Team.*

THE COLOURS OF THE NBA

ATLANTA HAWKS
Franchise history Joined NBA as Tri-Cities Blackhawks in 1949-50, became Milwaukee Hawks in 1951-52, became St. Louis Hawks in 1955-56, became Atlanta Hawks in 1968-69
NBA titles Won NBA Championship in St. Louis 1958
Ones to watch Stacey Augmon, Steve Smith, Mookie Blaylock

BOSTON CELTICS
Franchise history Charter member in 1946-47
NBA titles Won NBA Championships in 1957, 1959, 1960, 1961, 1962, 1963, 1964, 1965, 1966, 1968, 1969, 1974, 1976, 1981, 1984 and 1986
Ones to watch Dee Brown, Dino Radja, Dana Barros

CHARLOTTE HORNETS
Franchise history Began as expansion team in 1988-89
NBA titles None
Ones to watch Alonzo Mourning, Larry Johnson, Tyrone "Muggsy" Bogues

CHICAGO BULLS
Franchise history Began as expansion team in 1966-67
NBA titles Won NBA Championships in 1991, 1992 and 1993
Ones to watch Michael Jordan, Scottie Pippen, Toni Kukoc

CLEVELAND CAVALIERS
Franchise history Began as expansion franchise in 1970-71
NBA titles None
Ones to watch Terrell Brandon, Tyrone Hill, Dan Majerle

DALLAS MAVERICKS
Franchise history Began as expansion team in 1980-81
NBA titles None
Ones to watch Jason Kidd, Jamal Mashburn, Jim Jackson

DENVER NUGGETS
Franchise history Joined league from ABA in 1976-77
NBA titles None
Ones to watch Dikembe Mutombo, Antonio McDyess, Mahmoud Abdul-Rauf

DETROIT PISTONS
Franchise history Joined NBA in 1948-49 as Fort Wayne Pistons, became Detroit Pistons in 1957-58
NBA titles Won NBA Championships in 1989 and 1990
Ones to watch Grant Hill, Joe Dumars, Otis Thorpe

GOLDEN STATE WARRIORS
Franchise history Charter member as Philadelphia Warriors in 1946-47, became San Francisco Warriors in 1962-63 and Golden State Warriors in 1971-72
NBA titles Won NBA Championships in Philadelphia in 1947 and 1956; won NBA Championship in Golden State in 1975
Ones to watch Joe Smith, Tim Hardaway, Latrell Sprewell

HOUSTON ROCKETS
Franchise history Began as expansion San Diego Rockets in 1967-68; moved to Houston for 1971-72
NBA titles Won NBA Championships in 1994 and 1995
Ones to watch Hakeem Olajuwon, Clyde Drexler, Robert Horry

INDIANA PACERS
Franchise history Joined league from ABA in 1976-77
NBA titles None
Ones to watch Reggie Miller, Rik Smits, Derrick McKey

LOS ANGELES CLIPPERS
Franchise history Buffalo Braves began as expansion franchise in 1970-71, became San Diego Clippers in 1978-79, moved to Los Angeles for 1984-85
NBA titles None
Ones to watch Lamond Murray, Pooh Richardson, Loy Vaught

LOS ANGELES LAKERS
Franchise history Joined NBA in 1948-49 as Minneapolis Lakers, became Los Angeles Lakers in 1960-61
NBA titles Won NBA Championships in Minneapolis in 1949, 1950, 1952, 1953 and 1954; won NBA Championships in Los Angeles in 1972, 1980, 1982, 1985, 1987 and 1988
Ones to watch Nick Van Exel, Cedric Ceballos, Vlade Divac

MIAMI HEAT
Franchise history Began as expansion team in 1988-89
NBA titles None
Ones to watch New coach Pat Riley, Glen Rice, Billy Owens

MILWAUKEE BUCKS
Franchise history Began as expansion team in 1968-69
NBA titles Won NBA Championship in 1971
Ones to watch Glenn Robinson, Shawn Respert, Vin Baker

MINNESOTA TIMBERWOLVES
Franchise history Began as
expansion team in 1989-90
NBA titles None
Ones to watch Kevin Garnett,
Isaiah Rider, Christian Laettner

NEW JERSEY NETS
Franchise history Joined league
from ABA in 1976-77 as New York
Nets, became New Jersey Nets in
1977-78
NBA titles None
Ones to watch Derrick Coleman,
Kenny Anderson, Ed O'Bannon

NEW YORK KNICKS
Franchise history Charter member
in 1946-47
NBA titles Won NBA Championships
in 1970 and 1973
Ones to watch Patrick Ewing,
John Starks, Charles Oakley

ORLANDO MAGIC
Franchise history Began as
expansion team in 1989-90
NBA titles None
Ones to watch Shaquille O'Neal,
Anfernee Hardaway, Horace Grant

PHOENIX SUNS
Franchise history Began as
expansion franchise in 1968-69
NBA titles None
Ones to watch Charles Barkley,
Kevin Johnson, Danny Manning

PORTLAND TRAIL BLAZERS
Franchise history Began as
expansion franchise in 1970-71
NBA titles Won NBA Championship
in 1977
Ones to watch Clifford Robinson,
Rod Strickland, Randolph Childress

PHILADELPHIA 76ERS
Franchise history Joined NBA as
Syracuse Nationals in 1949-50,
became Philadelphia 76ers in 1963-64
NBA titles Won NBA Championship
in Syracuse in 1955 and in
Philadelphia in 1967 and 1983
Ones to watch Shawn Bradley, Jerry
Stackhouse, Clarence Weatherspoon

SACRAMENTO KINGS
Franchise history Joined NBA in
1948-49 as Rochester Royals,
became Cincinnati Royals in 1957-58,
became Kansas City-Omaha Kings in
1972-73, became Kansas City Kings
in 1975-76, became Sacramento
Kings in 1985-86
NBA titles Won NBA Championship
in Rochester in 1951
Ones to watch Mitch Richmond,
Brian Grant, Walt Williams

SAN ANTONIO SPURS
Franchise history Joined league
from ABA in 1976-77
NBA titles None
Ones to watch David Robinson,
Sean Elliot, Avery Johnson

SEATTLE SUPERSONICS
Franchise history Began as
expansion team in 1967-68
NBA titles Won NBA Championship
in 1979
Ones to watch Shawn Kemp,
Gary Payton, Detlef Schrempf

TORONTO RAPTORS
Franchise history Began as
expansion team in 1995-96
NBA titles None
Ones to watch Damon Stoudamire,
Alvin Robertson, Willie Anderson

UTAH JAZZ
Franchise history New Orleans Jazz
joined league as expansion team in
1974-75, moved to Utah for 1979-80
NBA titles None
Ones to watch Karl Malone,
John Stockton, Jeff Hornacek

VANCOUVER GRIZZLIES
Franchise history Began as
expansion team in 1995-96
NBA titles None
Ones to watch Bryant Reeves,
Lawrence Moten, Greg Anthony

WASHINGTON BULLETS
Franchise history Began as
expansion team Chicago Packers in
1961-62 season, became Chicago
Zephyrs in 1962-63, became
Baltimore Bullets in 1963-64 season,
became Capital Bullets in 1973-74
season and Washington Bullets in
1974-75
NBA titles Won NBA Championship
in 1978
Ones to watch Chris Webber,
Juwan Howard, Calbert Cheaney

facing page: *Second coming: When prodigal son Michael Jordan returned from his brief fling with baseball, the Bulls went from marginal team to championship contender.*
right: *Even when taking a breather, Jordan closely studies the flow of the play.*
far right: *Dynamite duo of Jordan and Scottie Pippen launched the Bulls to three NBA Championships.*

Everyone who comes away from an NBA game will recall a moment when he or she connected with the action. Closeups on the giant, ultra-clear television screens make the arenas seem like living rooms. The seats that border the playing surface are unheard of in other venues. They afford a chance to look into the eyes of the players, to see the strain of competition and the enthusiasm they have for the game.

Possessing the grace of gazelles in full flight, there can be little argument that the men who populate NBA rosters are indeed among the greatest athletes in the world. They play at a breakneck speed. Much of the game is played off the floor in mid-air, twisting and turning and pausing and shooting and rebounding in defiance of the laws of gravity. They bang big, muscled bodies under the basket. The game is as physical as it is fast.

As a total package, the NBA offers an unparalleled combination of superlative athletes and intense drama that makes it the most exciting game of our time.

"We happen to have a sport that happens to have the best athletes in the world, and you see them more intimately than in many other sports," Stern says. No helmets, no long sleeves,

no long pants, and the best seat in the house is one that's liable to find you with an athlete in your lap.

And the person sitting in your lap could very well be one of the game's stars who has dominated the league since its inception. From George Mikan through Wilt Chamberlain and Julius Erving to the greats of today, the league has always had marquee players who have been called upon to carry the banner for the league. There are few sports fans who don't know who David Robinson is, fewer still who wouldn't recognize Charles Barkley or Shaquille O'Neal or Scottie Pippen, and especially Michael Jordan. It is a star-driven league, and there have never been more stars.

The brightest star by far is still Jordan, the basketball-player-turned-baseball-player-turned-basketball-player whose tongue-flapping, gravity-defying skills have captured the imagination of every person who has ever seen him play. His flights of fancy from the free-throw line have enraptured an entire generation of young sports fans. His effortless drives down the lane defy description. Fans are left with mouths agape, commentators struggle to find suitable adjectives, and even opponents marvel at his brilliance.

following pages: *Rising above the Charlotte Hornets, Michael Jordan soars to the basket.*

left: *Heir ascendant: Since winning Rookie-of-the-Year honours in 1993, Shaquille O'Neal has soared to headliner status on the NBA marquee. His Magic prevailed over Jordan's Bulls in the 1995 playoffs.* right: *Shaq attaq: Shaq's backboard-rattling dunks propelled him to the NBA scoring title in 1994-95.*

Off the court, the multi-talented Shaq is also a rap musician and a budding actor. His mammoth stature and infectious grin have made him second only to Michael Jordan in endorsement contracts.

Jordan was one of the first to bring a truly amazing grace to the broadening NBA stage. At just six foot six, he can seemingly fly to the basket; his hang time is unprecedented. Sure, people in the past could jump, but few can take off from the free-throw line like Jordan, stay in the air for what seems to be an eternity and throw the ball down with grace and style. His efforts in the NBA's Slam Dunk competition during All-Star breaks were truly memorable and showcased his athletic grace in the perfect forum – centre stage, with no one else on the court.

During games, from his guard position he can sky over opponents who dare to sit back and challenge him to come to the basket. If someone comes out to play him up-close, he uses his spectacular first-step quickness to beat them to the basket.

His unique talents have set the parameters all other guards try to match these days. In order to equal Jordan – and no one else has succeeded – players have been forced to get quicker, jump higher and stretch their athletic limits. The prototypical shooting guard has been redesigned in Jordan's image.

Tipping the other end of the scale is O'Neal, all seven feet and 301 pounds of him. He blasts past opponents to the net and dunks with a ferocity few thought possible. He plays the big man's game, hard, tough, in-your-face, take-no-prisoners. One of the most marvellous physical specimens ever to play the game, he stands on the verge of a career that could dwarf the efforts of all other big men.

O'Neal, who averaged 29.3 points and 11.4 rebounds per game in the 1994-95 season, has taken his game to new heights in just three seasons in the NBA. Where he was once just a dunker and an intimidating physical presence, he has since added short jump hooks and fall-away baseline jumpers to his arsenal, making him all the more dangerous. If he ever becomes even an average foul shooter, his scoring totals could soar.

In a bygone era Bill Russell had his Wilt Chamberlain. Today, O'Neal has a trio of centres who provide a constant challenge and give the Orlando Magic pivot a standard against which his developing game can be measured.

acing page: *Summit meeting: Shaq and Hakeem Olajuwon tip off at centre court at Houston's Summit arena during last year's finals.* top he Dream: *Hakeem Olajuwon is considered by many to be the best in the game today.* bottom left: *Olajuwon drives around David Robinson f the San Antonio Spurs.* bottom right: *Underdogs from the start of the 1995 playoffs, the Rockets upset teams with the best four records n the regular season (Utah, Phoenix, San Antonio and Orlando) on their way to defending their NBA Championship.*

At the top of this group is the Nigerian-born Hakeem Olajuwon, who has carried the Houston Rockets to two consecutive NBA titles. "The Dream," as he's known, has starred in the NBA for more than a decade after gaining national recognition on the University of Houston's "Phi Slamma Jamma" teams. He's become the most complete centre in the game. At seven feet, 255 pounds, he runs the floor like a guard, has the silky smooth turnaround jump shot of a forward, and was the league's Most Valuable Player and Defensive Player of the Year in 1994, as well as the MVP of the NBA Finals back-to-back in 1994 and 1995.

Rounding out the quartet of established, dominant centres are David "The Admiral" Robinson of the San Antonio Spurs, and Patrick Ewing of the New York Knicks – teammates on the 1992 Dream Team, and fierce competitors on the NBA court.

Robinson, a six-year NBA veteran, got off to a delayed start on his career, spending two years in the U.S. Navy after graduating from the Naval Academy in 1987. It hasn't slowed him down much, as he has been on the Western Conference All-Star team each of his six seasons. He is a mobile centre, able to bang inside or play outside, giving defenders fits.

While Olajuwon has two NBA titles, and O'Neal and the Magic appear to be on the verge of a possible dynasty, Robinson has piled up some impressive individual credentials in San Antonio. He was the league's leading scorer in the 1993-94 season, averaging 29.8 points per game and solidifying his hold on the title with a brilliant 71-point effort against the Los Angeles Clippers on the final day of that regular season. In 1994-95, Robinson was the regular season MVP, averaging 27.6 points per game and appearing in 81 of the 82 regular season contests. The only thing he hasn't done is win an NBA title, but the Spurs enter each season as one of the favourites for the Western Conference crown.

Patrick Ewing has been the acknowledged leader of the New York Knicks and a force in the NBA since the day he left Georgetown University. Ewing lacks only an NBA Championship to put the icing on an illustrious career. A classic back-to-the-basket centre, he battles inside with ferocity on defence and is the go-to man on the New York offence. His turnaround jump shot has become among the best in the game.

far left: *Very emotional and animated on the court, Alonzo Mourning is the Charlotte Hornets' leading rebounder and a fierce competitor.*
left: *Strength against strength: When Shaq and Nugget's Dikembe Mutombo meet under the basket, it's a classic confrontation of the league's best offensive player against one of its best on defence.*
facing page: *A standout since winning Rookie-of-the-Year honours in 1990, David Robinson is the heart and soul of the San Antonio Spurs. In 1994-95 he led his team to the best regular season record – 62 wins and 20 losses.*

top (left to right): *Assistant coaches Mike Krzyzewski and Lenny Wilkens; Michael Jordan, Larry Bird, Magic Johnson, Chris Mullin, Clyde Drexler, John Stockton, P. J. Carlesimo.* **bottom:** *Scottie Pippen, Christian Laettner, Patrick Ewing, Head Coach Chuck Daly, David Robinson, Karl Malone, Charles Barkley.*

THE DREAM TEAM

The decision to allow NBA professionals to compete in the 1992 Summer Olympic Games provided the NBA and the sport with a global opportunity to spread the gospel of basketball, and the worldwide congregation soaked it up.

Magic, Michael and Larry; Sir Charles, The Admiral and The Mailman; Ewing, Pippen, Drexler, Stockton, Mullin and Laettner. They were members of that Dream Team, and they did more for the game through the 1992 Barcelona Olympics than any team had done for a sport at any time in the past.

"Some day, they're liable to talk about Before Dream Team and After Dream Team," NBA Commissioner David Stern says when talking about the impact the collection of stars will have on the worldwide acceptance of the sport. "It was the defining moment on the global basketball scene. It made Olympic basketball one of the pillars of Olympic competition, and it wasn't that way before the Dream Team."

The scene whenever the Dream Team played was incredible. Star-struck fans cheered from the far-flung reaches of Portland's Memorial Coliseum, where the team played the qualification event, to the top rows of the arena in Barcelona, Spain, the site of the Olympic tournament itself. The players spent the pre-Olympic period ensconced in Monte Carlo, a perfect location befitting basketball royalty. Public appearances were as one would expect – a mob scene of kids and adults trying to get close to heroes they had never before seen in person. A stroll by Charles Barkley down the jam-packed Las Ramblas tourist track in Barcelona was nothing more than a Royal Walkabout conducted by one of the Kings of the Court. At the opening ceremonies in Barcelona, Magic Johnson was mobbed by fellow athletes.

In addition to taking the game to unprecedented heights in popularity, the all-star collection of players took the game to new levels on the floor.

The Dream Team was the perfect basketball machine, the gifted Johnson at point guard directing an awesome offence with his array of no-look passes and fast-break baskets. He could dish off to the high-flying Jordan, hit Bird or Mullin in the corner for a three-pointer or catch Pippen or Malone or Drexler trailing the break. The team could pound it inside to Ewing or Robinson, neither of whom was ever guarded by a player of similar skills. The Dream Team won its games at the Olympics by an average margin of 43.8 points and scored 117.9 points per game. The closest anyone came was in the gold medal game when Croatia – with NBA regulars Dino Radja and Toni Kukoc – stayed within 32 points, a moral victory of sorts.

SALARY CAPS
AND THE DRAFT LOTTERY

They are two uniquely NBA processes that allow the league to stand out from all other professional sports organizations. They exist to promote some sense of parity among the member clubs, and how they are managed goes a long way in determining a franchise's fate. They are the salary cap and the draft lottery, and they're as important as shooting and ball-handling in the grand scheme of things.

The cap sets a specific dollar total – which changes year to year depending on team and league revenues – that can be spent on player salaries. It will crack the $20-million barrier in the 1995-96 season. Every team must manage the cap to keep the players it wants and go after the ones it desires. There are ways to manoeuvre within the cap that make this task even more important. It is a complicated procedure that teams are always thinking about when they are restructuring the contracts of players they already have or are negotiating with free agents they want.

The Grizzlies and Raptors are limited by their expansion agreements to spending just two-thirds of the league cap in their first year, three-quarters in their second and then the full amount in their third season.

While the salary cap is an exercise in advanced bookkeeping, the draft lottery is easier to understand, and plays a key role in the have-nots of the league hoping to become the haves. And, in typical NBA fashion, it has become an event. Each of the teams that misses the playoffs has a chance to win the lottery and choose the first overall pick in that year's draft. The nationally televised lottery is weighted so that the team with the worst record has the best chance of winning. However, if either Vancouver or Toronto wins the lottery before 1999, they will be moved to second in the draft and the second place team gets the first pick. If they finish one-two, the third place lottery team is the lucky winner.

The lottery was invented in 1985 to ensure that once teams had been eliminated from the playoff race, their drafting position would not be solely affected by their final record. Patrick Ewing of Georgetown University was the first lottery pick in history, and has gone on to greatness with the Knicks. The best lottery luck so far has belonged to the Orlando Magic, who won in both 1992 and 1993. With the first year's pick, they chose Shaquille O'Neal of Louisiana State University, and took Chris Webber of Michigan (above) the next season, dealing the latter to Golden State for Penny Hardaway. With O'Neal and Hardaway, Orlando vaulted ahead of many established teams to become a serious contender for the NBA title.

As centres become the focal point of many teams, there are other contenders trying to join O'Neal, Olajuwon, Robinson and Ewing in the superstar category. Two in particular are not that far away.

Alonzo Mourning of the Charlotte Hornets, the smallest of this group at six foot 10, has made big strides in the NBA after leaving Georgetown University only three seasons ago. Mourning, who is an NBA national spokesman against child abuse, is developing an intense rivalry with O'Neal, buoyed by the fact they play in the same conference and see each other four times a season. "Zo," who has twice led the Hornets to post-season appearances, paced the team in scoring and rebounding in the 1994-95 season, and seems destined for future greatness.

Another of those Georgetown greats is Denver's Dikembe Mutombo, a native of Zaire who is one of the game's pre-eminent defenders. A brilliant shot-blocker whose defensive skills are similar to those of Russell in his era with the Celtics, Dikembe Mutombo Mpolondo Mukamba Jean Jacque Wamutombo is becoming one of the most feared centres in the league.

In 1994-95, he led the league in shotblocking, and was second in rebounds per game – trailing only Dennis Rodman and placing ahead of Shaquille O'Neal.

facing page: *For the past decade, the New York Knicks' offence has revolved around Patrick Ewing's strong low post play.*

left: *A perennial league leader in shotblocking, Denver Nuggets' Mutombo is considered one of the top defenders in the league.* right: *Alonzo Mourning throws down a ferocious reverse jam.* facing page: *At six foot nine, Larry Johnson may tower over five-foot-three Tyrone "Muggsy" Bogues, but make no mistake, Bogues is the floor leader for the Charlotte Hornets.*

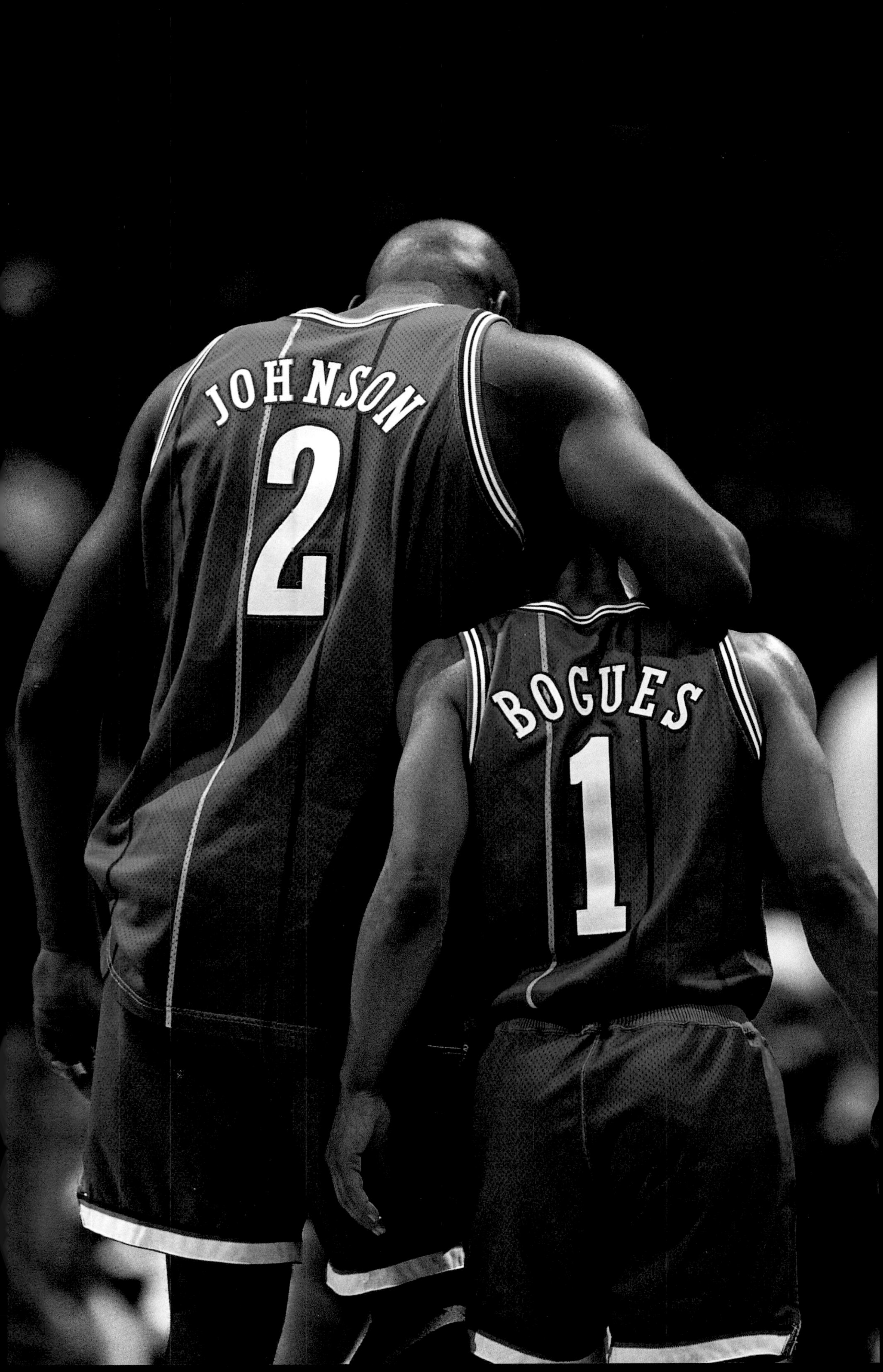
JOHNSON
2
BOGUES
1

ELITE FEET

They are the backbones of multi-million dollar businesses, they are fashion statements and important parts of worldwide marketing efforts.

They are basketball shoes and they are much, much more than footwear.

In the days of yore, the shoes worn by basketball stars were simple, black canvas, cut high above the ankles and adorned with nothing but eyelets for the laces.

Today, they are space-age high-tech pieces of equipment, delicately balanced for weight, support and arch support. They are also, of course, designed to catch the eyes and pocketbooks of teenagers and their parents all across the world. Shoe contracts can surpass playing contracts for some of today's NBA players and most advertising campaigns include a player-spokesman. Shoes have become an integral part of the game and the business these days. And they've provided a few interesting moments of late:

Great Moments in Footwear I: Michael Jordan is fined $5,000 for wearing white sneakers with black trim rather than black sneakers with white trim as the rest of his Chicago Bulls teammates do during the 1994-95 season.

Great Moments in Footwear II: Dennis Rodman incurs the wrath of San Antonio Spurs coach Bob Hill and a couple of teammates for taking off his shoes and lying on the floor, after being lifted from a playoff game last year.

Great Moments in Footwear III: Scottie Pippen, in one of the most memorable moments of sartorial splendour, is named the Most Valuable Player of the 1994 All-Star Game after scoring 29 points bedecked in a pair of the most garish red shoes known to man. "I definitely think it was the shoes. I think everybody was looking at my feet and I was able to shoot the ball well," he joked.

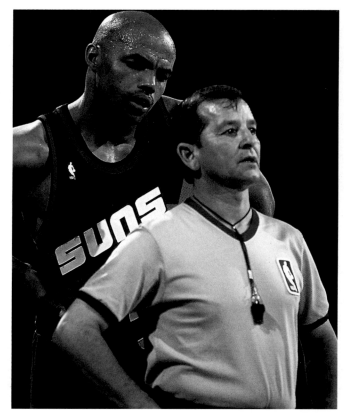

*All hail the Sun King! On offence, defence or in the media,
Phoenix Suns' Charles Barkley is never afraid to let his emotion
show. You never have to guess what Sir Charles is feeling.*

far left: *Phoenix point guard Kevin Johnson's lightning-quick first step leaves defenders flailing in his wake.*
left: *Three-point bomber "Thunder Dan" Majerle takes his aggressive driving style to the Cleveland Cavaliers for the 1995-96 season.*

Two of the most gifted and colourful players of all time are plying their trade in today's NBA, and people watch them as much for what they might say as for what they might do. Charles Barkley of the Phoenix Suns and Dennis Rodman of the Chicago Bulls are a couple of basketball-playing iconoclasts who are as unpredictable off the court as they are on it.

Barkley has electrified the NBA since leaving from Auburn University in 1984. Well-spoken, but ever outspoken, the six-foot-five forward remains a highly quotable figure who is never shy about speaking his mind. Although many of his off-court actions and comments have given him a rebellious image, Barkley also works silently behind the scenes helping the less fortunate, visiting hospitals and doing courtless hours of anonymous charity work. He is an enigma whose public persona does not reveal the man within.

On the court, Barkley is one of the game's greats. Despite his relative lack of height, he is one of the best rebounders in the game and a scoring machine who mixes it up with bigger foes every night. He has made the Suns a legitimate NBA title contender since being traded from Philadelphia, helping Phoenix reach the Finals against Chicago in 1993.

His drive to win manifests itself in many ways. He's not afraid to take both referees and teammates to task for mistakes in crucial games.

Barkley came out of college as the "Round Mound of Rebound," with tons of potential and what looked like an appetite to match. He worked on his game with his typical ferocity and culminated his development by being named the league's Most Valuable Player in 1993, his first season with the Suns. Barkley has said that he harbours hopes of a political career after his playing days are done, perhaps as governor of his home state of Alabama. Barkley in a government leadership role would be an interesting spectacle.

If colourful is the figurative adjective we use to describe Barkley, it's a literal description of Rodman, the man of many hair hues. While no one questions his abilities – a two-time NBA champion with the Detroit Pistons, one of the best rebounders the game has ever seen, with four straight NBA rebounding titles to prove it – he is as famous for his behaviour off the court, and that sometimes takes away from true appreciation for the gifts he has as a player. At just six foot eight, "The Worm," as he is known, battles bigger, stronger men for rebounds and nearly always wins. Unselfish almost to a fault at the offensive end of the court, Rodman often waits patiently on the wing for his teammates to run plays. But, once the ball hits the backboard or basket, he pounces like a lion on raw meat. He thinks every loose ball is his, and often it is.

Rodman is likely to show up with red hair one day, gold hair the next, green the day after that in his march to his own personal drummer. His pierced body, many and varied tattoos and personality have given him a special place in the NBA world. He has dated pop singer Madonna, was a presenter at the 1995 MTV awards, and reaches a hip, younger, non-traditional basketball audience. As Toronto Raptors Coach Brendan Malone, who was an assistant with the Pistons during Rodman's tenure, once said: "I'd like to get inside his head and see how he sees the world. But not for long, mind you."

That Rodman played on the same team with the conservative David Robinson was one of the great and intriguing mixes of personalities in all of sports. However, their diverse work ethics and comportment cost "The Worm" his employment in San Antonio just before the season began when he was dealt

to the Chicago Bulls in a giveaway for backup centre Will Perdue. Now he must fit in with Michael Jordan and the rest of the Bulls in Chicago. "It's a decision that's important to the franchise. We felt we had to weigh it out, think about it. I got to know a little about Dennis, that he's overcome a lot of odds. He's an awful strong individual and I'm confident he will take himself out of situations that have been tough for him his whole life," was how Chicago coach Phil Jackson summed up the deal.

Basketball is, and always will be, a team game in which five players working in symphony are necessary for victory. While a single star may capture the imagination of the fans, true success comes from teamwork – a great outside shooter with a dominant inside player, speed combined with strength, great starters with an excellent bench. Teams that have won in the past, and will win in the future, are finely tuned machines working absolutely in sync.

There are several sets of teammates in today's NBA who play off each other and complement each other's talents so well that the sum is far greater than the individual parts.

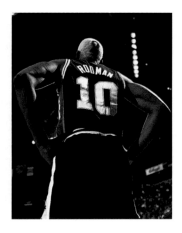

far left: *Free spirit: Dennis Rodman will tell fans what he's thinking after any play – good or bad.*
left: *The many hues of Dennis Rodman; this time it's blond.*
facing page: *A two-time NBA Defensive Player of the Year, Rodman grabs a rebound in his signature style.*

left: *Still near the top of his game after 10 years in the league, Karl Malone is the game's premier power forward.* top right: *Teammate John Stockton, the NBA's all-time assists leader, drives on the Magic.* bottom right: *Jazz combo: In Stockton and Malone Utah boasts one of the best guard-forward combinations ever.*

Karl Malone and John Stockton of the Utah Jazz are a perfect illustration of teammates working to near perfection. Ever since Malone was picked in the first round of the 1985 draft (a year after Stockton was taken in the first round of the 1984 draft), the duo has been working as one.

The powerful Malone, nicknamed "The Mailman" because he always delivers, is the all-time leading scorer in Jazz history, thanks mainly to Stockton, who is the career-assists leader in the NBA. A six-foot-nine forward, who also leads the Jazz in career rebounding, field goals made and attempted, and free throws made and attempted, Malone is one of the quiet superstars of the league, which has as much to do with the relatively small media market he plays in than anything else. He made a huge impact on the Dream Team at the Barcelona Olympics, and will play again on the team at the 1996 Atlanta Olympics.

But Malone without Stockton is nearly incomprehensible to NBA fans, so linked are the two. Stockton, like Malone a Dream Teamer in 1992, and in 1996 as well, passed Magic Johnson last season to take over the NBA career lead in assists. The six-foot-one graduate of tiny Gonzaga University is one of the most unselfish players in the game, always looking to make the great pass, a pass that often ends with a dunk or a layup for Malone.

THE COMMISSIONERS

From the time it was the Basketball Association of America with 11 teams anchored on the eastern seaboard, until a time when its players and teams are familiar and appreciated on every corner of the earth, only four men have held the NBA's mantle of command.

David Stern (above), Larry O'Brien, J. Walter Kennedy and Maurice Podoloff have been responsible for overseeing the transformation of the NBA from its origins in 1946 through to the present day. Generally considered the most savvy of all the commissioners of major sports leagues today, Stern began his tenure in 1984 after being the league's general counsel and vice president in charge of business and legal affairs. His time at the helm has been one of unprecedented popularity of the game.

Stern took over from Larry O'Brien, who served from 1975 to 1984. One of O'Brien's major tasks was helping speed along the merger between the NBA and the upstart American Basketball Association. O'Brien's ties to the political world – he was chairman of the Democratic party and an advisor to John F. Kennedy – helped immensely as the league was able to obtain approval from Congress for the 1976 union.

The biggest growth spurt in league history came under the eyes of J. Walter Kennedy, who was in charge from 1963 to 1975 and watched the league double in size from nine to 18 teams.

The task of getting the fractured basketball community to work for the common good in the infancy of the Basketball Association of America and the NBA fell to Maurice Podoloff, who guided the ship from 1946 to 1963. Podoloff was a Yale-educated lawyer born in Czarist Russia who had the necessary sports expertise when the league came calling. His connections were invaluable – he had been president of the American Hockey League, and his family owned New Haven Arena in Connecticut.

Podoloff convinced teams from the Midwest-based National Basketball League to join forces with the BAA in the late 1940s, a move that solidified the sport's base and set the stage for the development that continues today.

following pages: *Karl Malone goes in strong against the Lakers.*

While there have been no NBA Championships for the duo to celebrate, they did enjoy a memorable day on the national stage in 1993 when they were named co-winners of the Most Valuable Player award in the NBA's All-Star Game, a game that was played on their home court in Salt Lake City.

While Malone and Stockton have been creating their Utah magic for a decade, a new guard-forward tandem is rising in the Pacific Northwest. Shawn Kemp and Gary Payton of the Seattle SuperSonics represent the new wave of teammates who fill highlight reels night after night.

Kemp, who was one of the big fan favourites of the Dream Team at the World Championship of Basketball in Toronto in 1994, is one of the most acrobatic forwards in the game today. Despite not having played college basketball – he spent one year at junior college but did not play – he is one of the crowd favourites wherever he plays, primarily due to the intense emotions he shows after his thundering dunks leave opponents stunned and wondering what just hit them. He is power personified, six foot 10 and 245 pounds of muscle barrelling over anyone who gets in his way.

His power is augmented by the lightning quickness of his teammate Payton. After four years in the league, Payton, a six-foot-four guard, is developing into one of the game's pre-eminent defenders, able to strip opponents of the ball time and time again with hands and feet as fast as light. A two-time All-Star, he is the perfect complement to Kemp, and together they give the SuperSonics one of the most impressive young duos in the game.

Adding to the Sonics' emergence as one of the NBA's best teams is forward Detlef Schrempf. A former two-time winner of the Sixth Man of the Year award at Indiana, Schrempf has blossomed into an all-star starting forward whose game has improved every year since arriving in Seattle. One of the NBA's great playmaking forwards and an adept ball-handler, Schrempf is also a constant threat from beyond the three-point line. He finished second only to Steve Kerr of Chicago in three-point field goal accuracy during the past season and has proved himself to be the Sonics' most consistent player, night in and night out.

Seattle SuperSonics pose a triple threat to opponents.
facing page: Sonics on-court leader Shawn Kemp posted top-10 numbers in field goal percentage and rebounding for the 1994-95 season. Here, he leaves the Mavericks flatfooted.
far left: Commanding presence of point guard Gary Payton leaves opponent's defence in tatters.
left: Three-point threat Detlef Schrempf turns the corner on the Knicks.

A Kidd's game: Dallas fans have something to cheer about. In the last three years the Mavericks have acquired an all-star-calibre trio of young hot shots: Jason Kidd, Jim Jackson and Jamal Mashburn. Kidd possesses an inspired awareness of the floor and selfless passing skills which help the Mavericks make the most of their scoring opportunities.

Youth is also being served in Dallas, where the Mavericks are trying to escape from years of oblivion, powered by a tremendous trio of young talent in Jason Kidd, Jimmy Jackson and Jamal Mashburn. For years, the Mavericks were among the laughing stocks of the league, but their resurgence is being led by these three rising stars, who helped the team improve their win total by 23 games last season.

Jason Kidd, co-winner with Detroit's Grant Hill of the league's Rookie of the Year award in 1994-95 (the first co-winners since Dave Cowens and Geoff Petrie in the 1970-71 season), is another gifted passer in the Magic Johnson-John Stockton vein. Kidd led the league in triple doubles (points, assists and rebounds) and dazzled fans, players and coaches alike. Shooting guard, Jimmy Jackson is a complete player both offensively and defensively, and last season, before an ankle injury put him out of commission, he was the highest scoring non-centre in the league. Emerging as one of the league's premier power forwards in only his second year in the NBA, Jamal Mashburn finished fifth in scoring last season with a 24.1 points per game average.

Just as Kidd, Jackson and Mashburn are trying to lead the Mavericks to respectability, the team of Tim Hardaway, Latrell Sprewell and Chris Mullin are trying to accomplish the same feat with the Golden State Warriors, a team plagued by injuries and dissension in the last few years. Now that the Chris Webber-Don Nelson personality clash has been resolved with the trade of Webber to the Washington Bullets and Nelson's departure to coach the Knicks, Hardaway, Sprewell and Mullin will have to be the key ingredients to a Warriors resurgence. Hardaway possesses one of the game's singularly greatest moves with his cross-over dribble. The sheer speed of the move, moving a defender one way and then brilliantly cutting back to the other, is astonishing and will be Hardaway's legacy to the game. Sprewell, despite being a six-foot-five guard, can dunk with the best of them, and his explosions to the basket are memorable. The veteran Mullin, one of the game's best pure shooters, took his game to the world stage with the Dream Team in Barcelona, and, in combination with the quickness of Hardaway and Sprewell, keeps teams who want to focus on the other two honest.

A trio of rising stars has pulled the Mavericks into playoff contention. **left:** All eyes are on Jason Kidd, consensus choice as a future superstar. **top right:** Power forward Jamal Mashburn shot a higher field-goal percentage than all-time greats Larry Bird and Charles Barkley did in their sophomore years. **bottom right:** Explosive guard Jimmy Jackson, teamed with Kidd, gives Dallas a potential Hall-of-Fame backcourt.

eft: *Latrell Sprewell twists for two. The volatile guard
ed Golden State scorers in 1994-95.* **right:** *MVP
ontender Scottie Pippen goes to the hoop with authority.*

right: *Determined veteran forward Chris Mullin hopes to lead the Warriors back to prominence.*
far right: *High-scoring point guard Tim Hardaway is the floor general for Golden State.*

The missing achievement in all of those sets of dominant teammates, however, is the ultimate goal – an NBA Championship. Neither Stockton and Malone, nor Kemp and Payton, nor Kidd, Jackson and Mashburn, nor Hardaway, Sprewell and Mullin have yet to get their teams to the top of the mountain.

One team player who has been to the summit and can't wait to get back there again is Scottie Pippen, the small forward/ guard of the Chicago Bulls. A three-time NBA champion, a member of the 1992 Dream Team and next year's U.S. Olympic team, and arguably the best all-around player in the league, Pippen led the Bulls in points, rebounding, assists and minutes played last year and has one of the most complete games in the league. At six foot seven, he can post up guards, is comfortable playing the point or off-guard, and can move up to forward with ease. There are very few players in the game who can defend him, and on the defensive end of the floor, he's a demon, quicker than many forwards he matches up with, and bigger than the guards he opposes.

He also has a perfect foil in Croatian-born teammate Toni Kukoc, a six-foot-11 forward with great passing skills who is becoming more adept at the NBA style of game with every game played. Kukoc, who was on the Croatian team that lost the 1992 Olympic gold medal game to Pippen and the Dream Team, was a legendary star of the Italian professional league before jumping to the NBA. After some growing pains, he is becoming the player everyone thought he would be when he was wooed away from Europe.

But Pippen will always be remembered for the role he played in the Chicago Bulls dynasty of the early 1990s, a dynasty led by Michael Jordan, but one that wouldn't have existed without the contributions of Pippen and Horace Grant, the tireless power forward who is now making the Orlando Magic everyone's pick as the next dominant team.

The Pippen-Jordan championship teams of 1990-91, 1991-92 and 1992-93 represented a continuation of the multi-championship teams established in the 1980s by the Boston Celtics and Los Angeles Lakers, and continued by Isiah Thomas and the Detroit Pistons in the last two years of the decade.

From the Bulls, the torch has been passed to the Houston Rockets, the NBA champions of the last two seasons. The all-around brilliance of centre Hakeem Olajuwon has been the key, but last season's championship would not have been won without the contribution of Clyde "The Glide" Drexler, obtained in mid-season from the Portland Trail Blazers. Drexler, a team-mate of Olajuwon's at the University of Houston, had a storied 11-year career with Portland but had never won a title. The sight of him standing on the floor amid the jubilation after the championship had been clinched was the crowning moment to a brilliant career.

But where will the next great team come from? With the wealth of burgeoning young talent spread throughout the league, that's an impossible question to answer, but there are a few solid bets out there.

The best chance is being given to the up-and-coming Orlando Magic, last season's losing finalists but a promising young team anchored by the imposing presence of Mr. O'Neal. But even the great Shaq can't accomplish the ultimate feat alone, and it is the supporting cast that gives rise to the optimism in central Florida.

facing page: *The Croatian sensation, versatile Toni Kukoc has found an NBA home in Chicago.* following pages, top: *Celtics and Magic square off in legendary Boston Garden.* following pages, bottom: *Home of the greatest dynasty in NBA history, the Garden saw its last game in spring 1995.*

THE CANADIANS

From three players who were in the league in its first year of existence to two playing the game today, the dozen Canadian-born men who have made it to the NBA run the gamut of skill and contribution. All have battled long odds to reach the pinnacle of their sport.

Rick Fox (left) and Bill Wennington (right) are two Canadians well versed in the ins and outs of life in the NBA, and played together for the Canadian National Team. Fox, a native of Toronto, was drafted by the Boston Celtics in 1991, and he was the first rookie to start opening night for the Celtics since Larry Bird in 1979. For Bill Wennington, the transition into the NBA was not so smooth. After six seasons as an under-valued player with Dallas and Sacramento, Wennington went to Italy to give his career a kick start. There he led his team to the Italian Championships. He returned to the NBA two years later and is now a strong and valued player with the Chicago Bulls.

For Mike Smrek, his seven years in the NBA left him with enduring memories – and two championship rings as the only Canadian-born player to ever win an NBA title, a feat he accomplished with the 1986-87 and 1987-88 Los Angeles Lakers, playing with Magic Johnson and Kareem Abdul-Jabbar, during the era known simply as Showtime.

Leo Rautins, who will serve as the TV colour analyst for Raptors games this winter, was another who made that quantum leap. A standout forward at Syracuse University, he was a first-round draft pick of the Philadelphia 76ers in 1983, at that time the first Canadian ever chosen in the first round of the draft.

Only five men have gone from the ranks of the Canadian university system to the NBA. Jim Zoet went from Lakehead University to the Detroit Pistons; Ron Crevier, from Montreal's Dawson College to Golden State and Detroit; while American-born Brian Heaney attended Acadia University and played with the Baltimore Bullets. Two of the three Canadians who played with the 1946-47 Toronto Huskies – Gino Sovran and Hank Biasatti – were graduates of Windsor's Assumption College.

The rest of the Canadians – Toronto's Rautins; Stewart Granger of Montreal; Lars Hansen of Port Coquitlam, B.C.; Bob Houbregs of Toronto and Vancouver's Norm Baker – all developed their skills at American schools, the breeding ground for NBA stars.

Dreams will always drive Canadians to U.S. colleges, where the level of play is consistently far better and where the NBA scouts turn their attention when assessing prospects. But these days, with the advent of the new Canadian franchises, there will be more Canadians dreaming those dreams than in the past.

Entertainment tonight! The NBA's celebrity status draws Hollywood's glitterati.
far left: Knicks super fan, film director Spike Lee, trades taunts and cheers from his regular courtside seat at Madison Square Garden.
left: Hollywood heavyweight Jack Nicholson faithfully follows the Lakers at Forum home games.

Gifted point guard Penny Hardaway, obtained from the Golden State Warriors for Chris Webber on a draft-night deal in 1993, is developing into the best at his position in the league. Hardaway combines a great shooting touch, great ball-handling skills and a maturity that belies his years. His skills complement O'Neal's physical domination of the game under the backboards, and with leadership provided by veteran forward Horace Grant the Magic are poised to take the final step.

There are a handful of other great, players looking for the right combination of teammates and chemistry that will allow them to challenge the league's elite squads. Among them is Reggie Miller of the Indiana Pacers, who took his team as far as the Conference Finals in 1995, finally getting past the substantial hurdle imposed by Patrick Ewing and the New York Knicks. Miller, a member of the 1994 Dream Team, is one of the most gifted three-point shooters to ever play the game and has a knack of hitting the big shot at the most crucial point of the game. In last year's playoffs, he scored eight points in the dying seconds of a game to beat the Knicks in one of the most impressive clutch performances ever witnessed. And the fact that it happened in Madison Square Garden in

front of diehard Knicks fans and movie director Spike Lee, the biggest Knicks fan of all, made it all the more exciting.

Waiting patiently in the wings is a group of exciting young players who hope to leave their mark on the league as the superstars of the 1990s.

"Big Dog," Milwaukee's Glenn Robinson, made a significant impact with the Bucks in his rookie campaign, and has the Milwaukee faithful thinking playoffs again. After a tremendous college career at Purdue, culminating with consensus NCAA Player-of-the-Year honours in 1994, Robinson led all NBA rookies in scoring.

But while the "Big Dog" is barking, he's not the only young Buck making some noise. Vin Baker, a rookie whose skills were questioned by some when he was chosen eighth overall in the 1993 draft from the lightly regarded University of Hartford program, has become a perfect partner for Robinson in an excellent Milwaukee front line. The six-foot-10 power forward started all 82 games for Milwaukee in 1994-95, averaging 17.7 points and 10.3 rebounds as he made his first appearance in an All-Star Game, and became one of the most pleasant surprises in the NBA.

top: Savvy veteran Clyde "The Glide" Drexler, here driving around the Magic's Nick Anderson, helped Houston Rockets repeat as NBA champions in 1995. bottom: Unstoppable point guard Penny Hardaway came to the Magic on a draft-day trade and has Orlando talking dynasty.

left: *Solid defender Horace Grant brings championship experience to the youthful Orlando Magic from his three NBA titles with Chicago.* right: *Explosive Indiana point guard Reggie Miller is a threat from inside or long distance. His Pacers are considered to be NBA champions in waiting.*

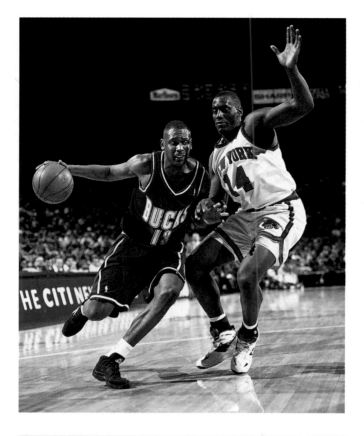

top left: *Highly touted rookie Glen "Big Dog" Robinson brings a complete game to the surging Milwaukee Bucks.* bottom left: *Robinson sets up for a two-handed power slam.* right: *All-star forward Vin Baker helps make the Milwaukee front line one of the best in the game.*

facing page: *Rookie sensation Grant Hill took the league by storm and is a fan favourite wherever he plays.*
left: *The future is bright for Grant Hill (left) and Jason Kidd, co-winners of the 1994-95 NBA Rookie-of-the-Year award.*

In Detroit, Grant Hill is a coach's delight as well as being one of the most engaging young players in the league. Just one year removed from a great career at Duke University, the son of former NFL running back Calvin Hill is ready to blossom. In his rookie season with the Pistons, Hill showed flashes of brilliance and a total game that includes taking the ball to the basket, the ability to pop out and hit jump shots, and a mature understanding of the nuances of the game. Coupled with a well-spoken nature, a clean-cut lifestyle and a sense of responsibility sadly lacking in some other young players, Hill has become a league favourite. Not only did he make the Eastern Conference All-Star starting line-up, he was the league leading vote-getter in fan balloting. No other rookie has ever achieved that milestone. The Pistons have high hopes for Hill as their leader for the future and a return to championship glory. His image is one of class, both on and off the court, making him the rare kind of athlete that seems to come along only once in a generation.

In Los Angeles, a resurgence of the Lakers is being led by one of the best young guards in the game, Nick Van Exel. At six foot one, the former Cincinnati star flourished under new coach Del Harris last year, and led the Lakers back to the playoffs, revitalizing the franchise along the way. A second-round pick of the 1993 draft who doesn't lack any confidence, he blossomed into an excellent scorer, averaging 16.9 points and 8.3 assists per game in 1994-95. Van Exel has a great supporting cast that includes rookie stand-out Eddie Jones, centre Vlade Divac and forward Cedric Ceballos.

Before being traded to Los Angeles, Ceballos never had the opportunity to truly showcase his talents. Playing a supporting role in Phoenix, it was difficult to crack the impressive cast of forwards in the Suns' line-up. The talent was there, but the numbers weren't in his favour. He has become an All-Star since being traded to the Lakers, and Jones, a former Temple star, was a strong contender for Rookie-of-the-Year honours in the 1994-95 season. Divac had his finest season as a pro in the 1994-95 season with career highs in scoring, blocks and assists. His assist total was the highest of all NBA centres and he was the only player in the league to have three 20-point, 20-rebound games last season.

top left: *Laker guard Nick "The Quick" Van Exel blows past Dennis Rodman.*
top right: *Lakers 10th pick overall in the 1994 NBA draft, Eddie Jones blossomed into the Rookie All-Star Game MVP.* bottom: *Working off a pick by Vlade Divac, Cedric Ceballos drives to the basket.*

*Sacramento scoring sensation Mitch Richmond en
route to another two against Milwaukee.*

In Sacramento, the long-suffering Kings fans are finally being rewarded with a much improved team. Led by shooting guard Mitch Richmond, the Kings now come to the court believing they can beat any team in the league. Richmond has represented the Kings in the All-Star Game for three straight years, winning the MVP award in last season's contest.

With the surprising emergence of rookies Brian Grant and Michael Smith, and solid play from third year man Walt Williams, youthful Sacramento is poised to return to the playoffs for the first time since 1986.

The contemporary NBA is flourishing: there are big men and small, deadly shooters and lightning-quick slashers, brilliant defenders and dominant rebounders. There are teams on the rise, players destined for greatness and rivalries developing that will be fought well into the next millennium.

The stunning growth over the last decade will be hard to match, but as the game branches out with expansion and an even greater world audience, the future looks bright indeed.

Some might argue that there has always been a Canadian flavour to the NBA. After all, James Naismith, the father of basketball, was born and raised in Canada. Maurice Podoloff, the league's first president, whose name graces the trophy awarded annually to the NBA's Most Valuable Player, was also a Canadian. Yet, until now, one key element was missing from the equation – Canadian fans have not had a team to call their own. But starting this season, the greats of the game will travel north to strut their finest across the hardwood.

In Vancouver, the sparkling new General Motors Place and an overwhelming sense of optimism await the Grizzlies as they take to the floor for their first season. Fans have rallied in record numbers to support their new franchise, looking forward to the day when a championship is within reach.

In a city used to superlatives, the Grizzlies are pledged to define the term, both through their effort on the court and in their contributions to the community that has welcomed them. At first, the road to success in the NBA may be hard, but even the greatest journey begins with a single step, and the Grizzlies are already hitting full stride.

THE

a b o v e : *Bearskin: Grizzlies' stylish uniforms – sporting a unique colour palette of Pacific turquoise, Bear bronze, Naismith red and black – are a hit with fans across North America.*

The excitement and tension were palpable in the Vancouver Grizzlies war room on the historic evening of

G R I Z Z L I E S

Wednesday, June 28, 1995. The assembled collection of basketball brains was about to embark on a momentous occasion, one which would shape the destiny of a $125 million U.S. investment for years to come.

Stu Jackson, the man who would speak the all-important words and ultimately make the crucial decisions in the following three hours, had brought together the men who had scoured North America looking for the consummate young basketball player to fit the team's needs.

It was draft night in the NBA and it was the biggest and most important event in the history of the team.

As the vice president of basketball operations and general manager of the expansion franchise, Jackson could feel the pressure. The right choice would start the Grizzlies on the path to NBA greatness in the years to come. The wrong choice would be a setback an expansion team can rarely afford.

But Jackson was confident he was about to make the correct pick. Drafting sixth – a right the Grizzlies had earned by winning a coin toss with the Toronto Raptors – Jackson knew he would get an impact player, a youngster around whom the foundation for the future could be built. He knew precisely who that player was, what he stood for and what he could accomplish.

Thousands of kilometres away, on a stage in the middle of Toronto's SkyDome, sat Jay Triano, the Grizzlies' Director of Community Relations, flanked by Director of Media Relations

Steve Frost. Triano took a phone call from Jackson, and passed the name on to a member of the NBA staff. Commissioner David Stern strode to the microphone and spoke the words which signalled a new era in Vancouver sports history.

"With the sixth selection in the 1995 NBA draft, the Vancouver Grizzlies select from Oklahoma State, Bryant Reeves."

In Vancouver, Stu Jackson looked around at Head Coach Brian Winters, Scouting Director Larry Riley and the rest of the staff and smiled the smile of a contented man. The foundation – a big, seven-foot foundation – has been laid with the drafting of Bryant "Big Country" Reeves.

There is a saying in the NBA that you can't teach height and no one knows better the truth in that wisdom than Jackson. As the youngest head coach hired in the history of the New York Knicks in 1988, he had seen first-hand the importance of a dominant presence in the middle. He had seen Patrick Ewing play night after night, had watched in the past few years as Hakeem Olajuwon, Shaquille O'Neal and David Robinson had turned the game back into a battle of the big men. He knew what the Grizzlies needed more than anything and he got it.

The making of an NBA centre: In a forest of big men, Reeves must add craft and guile to his natural height advantage. In pre-season play, he worked to develop his all-around skills. left: *Reeves, shooting against the Raptors' Willie Anderson at the Naismith Cup exhibition game, October 21, 1995, in Winnipeg.* top right: *Setting up in the low-post position versus Chris Dudley of the Portland Trail Blazers.* bottom right: *Battling for position against Sean Rooks of the Minnesota Timberwolves.*

"Our decision to draft Bryant reflects the premium we've placed on a big centre," Jackson said that evening after the euphoria of draft night had abated somewhat. "Bryant gives us size, excellent shooting skills, solid passing, soft hands and, perhaps most important, a yeoman's work ethic."

The Grizzlies used their second-round pick to select shooting guard Lawrence Moten from Syracuse University. Moten finished his standout college career as the all-time leading scorer in Big East Conference history, and the Grizzlies are looking for him to provide scoring punch from the backcourt.

In the hands of Reeves and Moten lies the future of the Vancouver franchise, but for the present, Jackson and his advisors needed some experienced NBA players, players who could take the floor when the Grizzlies' first season opens in November 1995 and give the team immediate credibility. On June 24 the NBA expansion draft allowed Vancouver to select the players who would help make up its opening night roster.

He got a point guard in Greg Anthony, a four-year veteran from the New York Knicks, with his first pick. Backing up Anthony at the point guard spot will be free agent Kevin Pritchard, the first player to be signed by the Grizzlies.

To fill the off-guard spot, Jackson took another couple of veterans, Byron Scott of Indiana and Gerald Wilkins of Cleveland, who missed the 1994-95 season with an injury but will be the steal of the draft if he's fully recovered. Kenny Gattison, no stranger to the expansion process having been an expansion pick of the Charlotte Hornets himself, was also taken, as was New Jersey centre Benoit Benjamin, who can help ease "Big Country" Reeves into the NBA wars. Blue Edwards came over from Utah, while young forward/centre Antonio Harvey was plucked from the Los Angeles Lakers; forward Doug Edwards was taken from Atlanta and forward Larry Stewart moved from the Washington Bullets to Vancouver.

"It felt like a sophisticated game of pickup and it was a lot more fun," Jackson said.

Even more than talent, Jackson wanted players who could handle the difficulties that come with playing on an expansion team. Wins are hard to come by for an expansion team, so the general manager wanted mature young men who could see the big picture. In Anthony, who will run the offence,

TORONTO RAPTORS

It was in 1990 that John Bitove, Jr. first considered the possibility of bringing the NBA to Toronto, and for the next few years he started meeting with NBA officials, eventually becoming a familiar face within the league and biding his time until expansion fever hit and he could strike.

And then his hand was forced.

A group led by construction magnate Larry Tanenbaum made a pre-emptive strike by sending a $100,000 deposit cheque to the league's head office early in 1993. Another group also came into play, led by concert magnates Bill Ballard and Michael Cohl, with the imposing presence of Magic Johnson on side.

By putting together a group that included broadcasting executive Allan Slaight, former Ontario premier David Peterson, the Bank of Nova Scotia and long-time family friend Phil Granovsky, Bitove had gathered a collection of influential and dedicated partners who were eager to tackle the work that lay ahead.

The resulting competition was intense. And then, on the night of September 30, 1993, Russ Granik, the deputy commissioner of the NBA, called to inform Bitove that he had won the biggest prize there was.

Bitove now had two years in which to construct a team and have it ready to play for the 1995-96 NBA season. There was still a lot of work ahead. For his most important hiring on the basketball side of the operation, Bitove turned to Isiah Thomas. He had been a student at Indiana University at the same time as Bitove, and had been a two-time NBA champion with the Detroit Pistons, and he was now to become the Raptors' first vice president of basketball operations.

So with Bitove having won the right to own the team in a hard-fought boardroom battle, with Thomas having won NBA championships in hard-fought basketball battles, the Raptors have a good start on becoming a gritty competitor in their inaugural season.

he appears to have one. "This team is on the upswing," Anthony said after being drafted. "They're just starting the journey up the mountain. There's an opportunity for me to be a part of that. You have to look at the high side of the possibilities."

Leading the Grizzlies up that mountain will be Stu Jackson. And he will be judged not on what he has done to date – however substantial – but on what he will do as the man in charge of the day-to-day operations of a fledgling NBA franchise. Still, the pressure doesn't faze him in the least.

Says Jackson at the end of another long day in his General Motors Place office: "This should be fun, it's expansion. I think Kenny Gattison (one of the team's picks in the expansion draft) put it best when he described his experience with the Charlotte Hornets. He said you've got to take this for what it's worth; it's a chance to work extremely hard and to have some fun."

Work hard and have fun. That's what Jackson has done since he took the Grizzlies job in late 1994. Building a team, being involved in every aspect of the development of the organization – from ticket selling to hiring a scouting staff, hiring a coach and negotiating for the services of professional athletes – has given Jackson a mountain of work he's just loved tackling.

top: *Point guard Greg Anthony will be called upon to run the offence for the Grizzlies, a role he previously handled for the New York Knicks.* **bottom:** *The offensive punch of shooting guard Byron Scott, a veteran of 12 NBA seasons, will help school the younger guards in how to play the position.*

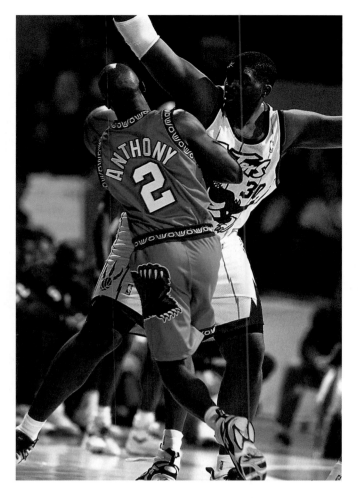

facing page: *Developing teamwork will make the Grizzlies offence thrive: Greg Anthony drives around a screen set by Antonio Harvey against Sacramento.* top left: *Greg Anthony passes around the Raptors' Oliver Miller.* top right: *Kenny Gattison sets up for a free throw.* bottom left: *Byron Scott goes airborne for a jumper against the Raptors.* bottom right: *"Big Country" Reeves and Larry Stewart attempt to thwart Trail Blazers' Arvyadas Sabonis' layup attempt.*

left: *Seven-foot centre Benoit Benjamin will match up strongly against other big men in the league. Here he lofts a hook shot over Christian Laettner of the Minnesota Timberwolves during pre-season.* right: *Aggressive ex-Laker forward Antonio Harvey throws down a big dunk versus Portland in the Grizzlies' first pre-season game.*

far left: *The Grizzlies will be looking for leadership from Byron Scott who brings championship experience, after winning three NBA titles with the Los Angeles Lakers.*
left: *At shooting guard, the Grizzlies have big plans for 10-year veteran Gerald Wilkins on both the offensive and defensive ends of the court.*

Since leaving the University of Oregon, where a serious knee injury ended a promising playing career in 1976, Jackson has been an assistant and the head coach of the Knicks, an assistant to NBA director of operations Rod Thorn, a computer salesman for IBM and the head coach of the Wisconsin Badgers. Through each of those incarnations, he's learned something, and the sum total of that knowledge has helped him make the Grizzlies an exceptional organization from top to bottom before the team ever takes to the floor.

"Working for Rod Thorn and the league office was one of the most rewarding career experiences I've had because it gave me an introduction into the inner workings of the league and the business of basketball," says Jackson. "I began to understand what characterized a good basketball operation and what characterized a bad operation."

And it is that understanding that has allowed Jackson to flourish in Vancouver. He has surrounded himself with exceptional people, including Brian Winters and Larry Riley. Each has a unique place in the Grizzlies organization and Jackson has made sure each has the latitude to do his job to the best of his abilities.

To hear his passion for the historic role he's playing is to marvel at his single-minded dedication.

"Being given the opportunity to start from the ground up in any professional sports organization is as attractive a situation as you can ask for. The challenge of helping be part of history in moving NBA basketball north of the border into Canada was one of particular interest to me. It was just the magnitude of the challenge, that was something I just couldn't resist."

While Jackson has all the tools necessary to develop the business side of the game, he started in the NBA at courtside, and it's part of his fabric that will never be diminished. He coached in the cauldron that is New York City, he coached in the high-stress of the top levels of the NCAA and he knows and loves the game. When he took over a Wisconsin Badger team in 1992, such distinguished basketball men as Rick Pitino and Don Nelson told him it was a dead end, he could accomplish little with a program that hadn't been to the NCAA tournament since 1947. "If people thought the job was that bad, I felt like I had to find a silver lining. It's like when you pick a stock. You've got to buy low," Jackson said in a *Sports Illustrated* article in 1994 – the same year he proved the

STARTING FIVE

Stu Jackson personally spearheaded the development of the Grizzlies' team uniforms and the court design at General Motors Place. Yet the Vancouver General Manager has been equally hands-on in shaping the Grizzlies community partnerships and social marketing with Tom Mayenknecht, Vice President, Communications and Public Relations, and Jay Triano, one of Canada's best and best-known basketball players and long-time head basketball coach at Simon Fraser University, who joined the team in mid-1995 as Director of Community Relations.

The Grizzlies proactive approach to community relations and their charitable foundation will be guided by a five-pronged plan that places the Grizzlies at the forefront of issues important to the social fabric of the city, province and country they represent.

The "Starting Five," as the initiatives are known, include educational and environmental issues that are as important to the Grizzlies front office as the basketball team.

The two "Backcourt" programs deal with sports and education, and include Grizzlies Futures, a $2 million endowment at the University of British Columbia, funded equally by the university and the NBA team. The money is used for a variety of purposes, from giving under-privileged kids the opportunity to compete in sports to, one day, granting young athletes scholarships to finance their shot at excellence. The educational portion in part deals with the NBA's superb Stay in School program, showing kids the importance of education and how it sets the stage for a bright future. The Grizzlies and UBC also intend to make scholarships available for excellence in academics.

The three "Frontcourt" programs take the Grizzlies to the forefront of environmental issues. The first confronts the external environment, and, as an example, provides funding to support British Columbia's Grizzly Bear Conservation Strategy.

The "internal" environment portion will assist children and hospitals, helping to fund vital research, preventative medicine and programs for children with disabilities.

Finally, the "family" environment initiatives will include such all-important issues as drug and alcohol awareness and a project which helps foster the caring kind of lifestyle the Grizzlies want to be known for.

The "Starting Five" will be as important to Grizzlies' community relations as they will be to the Grizzlies Foundation, part of Orca Bay charities.

naysayers wrong and took the Badgers to the NCAA tournament. Giving up that career on the bench was the most difficult part of accepting the Vancouver job.

Off the court, Jackson has the Grizzlies moving forward in an unrelenting march to success. The league-mandated target of 12,500 season-tickets was a monumental task for the team to accomplish but it did, in no small part because of Jackson's ability to stir up excitement among the people of Vancouver.

"We're at a point now where, organizationally, we have so many different areas coming together – be it sponsorship, suite holders, ticket holders, the entertainment-game operation side of it, the communications side of it, the media relations side of it, scouting, coaching – and to have played a part in it is very rewarding. Four or five years down the road when we're a solid, established club you can look back and know you've had a part in creating that, I think that's the greatest of rewards."

Fortunately for Jackson, the process of reaping those rewards will begin on schedule this fall. After much of the preparatory work had been done, after Reeves had been selected, after the expansion draft process had been completed and just when the focus was going to be placed on the game, the rug was momentarily pulled out from the basketball side of the operations.

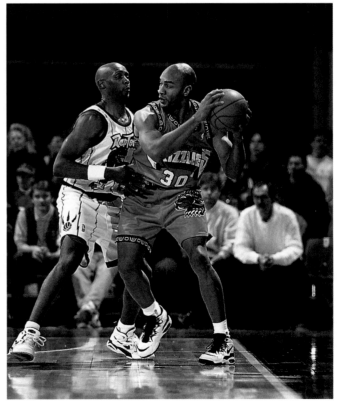

top: *Power forward Kenny Gattison, here battling against the Raptors for position under the boards, will contribute leadership and stability.* bottom left: *A strong offensive contributor in pre-season play, Blue Edwards shoots a three-pointer over Chris Whitney of the Raptors during the Naismith Cup.* bottom right: *Edwards considers his options against Raptors defender Alvin Robertson.*

left: *Former Washington Bullet Larry Stewart leaves defenders flailing as he soars to the hoop against the Timberwolves.* **top right:** *Free agent acquisition, Litterial Green leads the Grizzlies' fast break versus Minnesota.* **bottom right:** *Benoit Benjamin backs in to the hoop against Raptors big man Oliver Miller.*

eft: *Defence will help the Grizzlies keep close enough to snatch victory: Antonio Harvey comes from*
nderneath the basket to block a Raptors scorinc chance. right: *Blue Edwards dunks aggressively*

The first work stoppage in NBA history, a two-month lockout which began on July 1, put all basketball operations on hold for the summer, a crucial time in the development of an expansion franchise.

Just when Jackson, his assistant general manager Noah Croom, Brian Winters, and Larry Riley and his scouting staff should have been beating the bushes for free-agent players and signing Reeves and Moten, everything stopped.

A rookie free-agent camp, which normally would have been held in early July, was called off. A planned entry in the Los Angeles summer league had to be cancelled.

To their credit, the NBA and its players' union solved the dispute without the loss of a single minute of training camp. A new six-year deal was signed in early September, allowing the Grizzlies to hold a rookie and free-agent camp before training camps opened on schedule October 6. Pre-season games against Portland, Sacramento, and Minnesota allowed the coaching staff to try out various combinations of players in search of the right mix. Then, on October 21, the Grizzlies met their expansion cousins from Toronto in the first annual Naismith Cup for pre-season bragging rights.

The Raptors were out of the gate quickest this time around, posting a 98-77 victory in front of 11,203 fans at the Winnipeg Arena. Despite missing injured shooting guard Gerald Wilkins and point guard Kevin Pritchard from their pre-season line-up, Coach Winters and the Grizzlies were disappointed with their first Naismith Cup performance, realizing much improvement lay ahead.

When the Grizzlies step out onto the court at magnificent General Motors Place for the first regular season home game, November 5, 1995, against the Minnesota Timberwolves, the games will count for something other than just pride. From that point on the Grizzlies will build upon the lessons they learn in their first season to ensure future success.

In a perfect world, dreams come true. Arthur Griffiths' ambitious dream of NBA basketball gracing a sparkling new showplace by the Pacific has become a reality. And based upon the track records of the Griffiths and John McCaw, the Vancouver Grizzlies are destined to be come a major power of the NBA in the young 21st century.

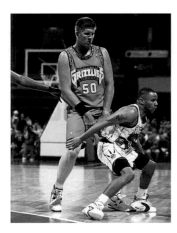
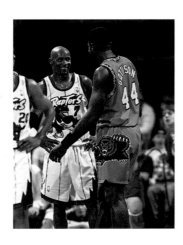

far left: *Futures collide: In the debut matchup between Canadian franchise first rounders, Bryant Reeves sets a pick on the Raptors' Damon Stoudamire.*
left: *Camaraderie and competitiveness go hand in hand in the NBA. Kenny Gattison of the Grizzlies and Alvin Robertson of the Raptors share a lighter moment during the Naismith Cup.*
facing page: *The chance to seize a piece of history as Naismith Cup action brought out the competitive best in both teams: the Grizzlies' Litterial Green and the Raptors' Carlos Rogers scramble for a loose ball.*

The Vancouver Grizzlies launched their inaugural pre-season campaign featuring the players listed on these pages.

GREG ANTHONY - GUARD

Six foot one
185 lbs.
New York Knicks
November 15, 1967
Four years in NBA

TEAM	G	FGM	FGA	PCT	3-PT	FG	PCT	FTM	FTA	PCT	REBS	AST	PPG
91-94 New York	232	560	1425	.393	60	245	.245	354	485	.730	495	1077	6.6
94-95 New York	61	128	293	.437	56	155	.361	60	76	.789	64	160	6.1
Career	293	688	1718	.400	116	400	.290	414	561	.738	559	1237	6.5
94-95 Playoffs	11	15	38	.395	7	23	.304	10	11	.909	10	15	4.3
Career Playoffs	63	103	272	.379	33	110	.300	52	82	.634	84	167	4.6

BYRON SCOTT - GUARD

Six foot four
200 lbs.
Indiana Pacers
March 28, 1961
12 years in NBA

TEAM	G	FGM	FGA	PCT	3-PT	FG	PCT	FTM	FTA	PCT	REBS	AST	PPG
83-94 LAL/Ind	834	5219	10630	.491	549	1481	.371	1963	2364	.830	2526	2399	15.5
94-95 Indiana	80	265	583	.455	79	203	.389	193	227	.850	151	108	10.0
Career	914	5484	11213	.489	628	1684	.373	2156	2591	.832	2677	2507	15.0
94-95 Playoffs	17	32	94	.340	9	34	.265	30	34	.882	25	16	6.1
Career Playoffs	175	919	1904	.483	130	328	.396	432	529	.816	524	379	13.7

ANTONIO HARVEY - FORWARD/CENTRE

Six foot 10
225 lbs.
Los Angeles Lakers
July 6, 1970
Two years in NBA

TEAM	G	FGM	FGA	PCT	FTM	FTA	PCT	REBS	AST	BLK	PPG
93-94 L.A. Lakers	27	29	79	.367	12	26	.462	59	5	19	2.6
94-95 L.A. Lakers	59	77	176	.438	24	45	.533	102	23	41	3.0
Career	86	106	255	.416	36	71	.507	161	28	60	2.9
94-95 Playoffs	3	0	0	.000	0	0	.000	1	0	0	0.0

KENNY GATTISON - FORWARD/CENTRE

Six foot eight
256 lbs.
Charlotte Hornets
May 23, 1964
Eight years in NBA

TEAM	G	FGM	FGA	PCT	FTM	FTA	PCT	REBS	AST	BLK	PPG
86-94 Pho/Cha*	448	1398	2666	.524	772	1180	.654	2138	413	301	8.0
94-95 Charlotte	21	47	100	.470	31	51	.608	75	17	15	6.0
Career	469	1445	2766	.522	803	1231	.652	2213	430	316	7.9
94-95 Playoffs	4	5	8	.625	5	8	.625	12	2	0	3.8
Career Playoffs	13	27	54	.500	14	29	.483	51	13	1	5.2

*Did not play in 87-88 due to injury.

GERALD WILKINS - GUARD

Six foot seven
218 lbs.
Cleveland Cavaliers
September 11, 1963
10 years in NBA

TEAM	G	FGM	FGA	PCT	3-PT	FG	PCT	FTM	FTA	PCT	REBS	AST	PPG
85-94 N.Y./Cle	717	4213	9157	.460	309	946	.327	1583	2116	.748	2317	1573	14.4
94-95 Did not play due to injury.													
Career	717	4213	9157	.460	309	946	.327	1583	2116	.748	2317	1573	14.4
Career Playoffs	50	276	616	.448	19	70	.271	93	117	.795	144	186	13.3

DOUG EDWARDS - FORWARD

Six foot seven
235 lbs.
Atlanta Hawks
January 21, 1971
Two years in NBA

TEAM	G	FGM	FGA	PCT	3-PT	FG	PCT	FTM	FTA	PCT	REBS	AST	PPG
93-94 Atlanta	16	17	49	.347	0	1	.000	9	16	.563	18	8	2.7
94-95 Atlanta	38	22	48	.458	0	1	.000	23	32	.719	48	13	1.8
Career	54	39	97	.402	0	2	.000	32	48	.667	66	21	2.0
Career Playoffs	1	0	0	.000	0	0	.000	0	0	.000	0	0	0.0

LARRY STEWART – FORWARD

Six foot eight
230 lbs.
Washington Bullets
September 21, 1968
Four years in NBA

TEAM	G	FGM	FGA	PCT	FTM	FTA	PCT	REBS	AST	BLK	PPG
91-94 Washington	160	612	1162	.527	379	496	.764	839	268	74	10.0
94-95 Washington	40	41	89	.461	20	30	.667	67	18	9	2.6
Career	200	653	1251	.522	399	526	.759	906	286	83	8.5

BENOIT BENJAMIN – CENTRE

Seven feet
265 lbs.
New Jersey Nets
November 22, 1964
10 years in NBA

TEAM	G	FGM	FGA	PCT	FTM	FTA	PCT	REBS	AST	BLK	PPG
85-94 LAC/Sea/ LAL/NJ	636	2993	6040	.496	1751	2434	.719	5013	963	1427	12.2
94-95 New Jersey	61	271	531	.510	133	175	.760	440	38	64	11.1
Career	697	3264	6571	.497	1884	2609	.722	5453	1001	1491	12.1
Career Playoffs	18	50	99	.505	45	58	.776	100	7	34	8.1

THEODORE "BLUE" EDWARDS – GUARD/FORWARD

Six foot four
228 lbs.
Utah Jazz
October 31, 1965
Six years in NBA

TEAM	G	FGM	FGA	PCT	3-PT FG	PCT	FTM	FTA	PCT	REBS	AST	PPG
89-94 Utah/Mil	339	1899	3741	.508	129 369	.350	729	955	.763	1461	775	12.0
94-95 Bos/Utah	67	181	393	.461	22 75	.293	75	90	.833	130	77	6.9
Career	456	2080	4134	.503	151 444	.340	804	1045	.769	1591	852	11.2
94-95 Playoffs	4	4	12	.333	1 1	1.000	0	0	.000	6	3	2.3
Career Playoffs	34	107	226	.473	5 16	.313	46	60	.767	103	44	7.8

KEVIN PRITCHARD – GUARD

Six foot three
185 lbs.
Free agent
July 18, 1967
Three years in NBA

TEAM	G	FGM	FGA	PCT	3-PT FG	PCT	FTM	FTA	PCT	REBS	AST	PPG
90-92 G.S./NY	73	104	263	.395	5 34	.147	76	95	.800	76	111	4.1
94-95 Phil/Mia	19	13	32	.406	2 8	.250	16	21	.762	12	34	2.3
Career	92	117	295	.397	7 42	.166	92	116	.793	88	145	3.6

ROOKIES

BRYANT REEVES – CENTRE

*First round,
  sixth overall*
Seven feet
292 lbs.
Oklahoma State
June 8, 1973

TEAM	G	FGM	FGA	PCT	FTM	FTA	PCT	REBS	AST	BLK	PPG
91-92 Okla. State	36	111	213	.521	69	109	.633	182	24	26	8.1
92-93 Okla. State	29	210	338	.621	145	223	.650	291	36	38	19.5
93-94 Okla. State	34	264	451	.585	185	311	.595	329	52	70	21.0
94-95 Okla. State	37	289	493	.586	219	310	.706	350	30	60	21.5
Career	136	874	1495	.585	618	953	.648	1152	142	194	17.4

LAWRENCE MOTEN – GUARD

*Second round,
  36th overall*
Six foot five
185 lbs.
Syracuse
March 25, 1972

TEAM	G	FGM	FGA	PCT	3-PT FG	PCT	FTM	FTA	PCT	REBS	AST	PPG
91-92 Syracuse	34	193	388	.497	45 140	.321	152	202	.752	192	63	18.2
92-93 Syracuse	29	191	404	.473	44 131	.336	92	141	.652	138	77	17.9
93-94 Syracuse	29	245	489	.501	50 176	.284	104	149	.698	135	66	22.2
94-95 Syracuse	29	209	455	.459	58 177	.328	113	152	.743	125	99	20.3
Career	121	838	1736	.483	197 624	.316	461	644	.716	590	305	19.3

1 9 9 5 - 9 6  s c h e d u l e

N O V E M B E R

3	Portland	7:00 p.m.
5	Minnesota	6:00 p.m.
7	Dallas	5:30 p.m.
8	San Antonio	5:30 p.m.
10	L.A. Clippers	7:30 p.m.
11	Seattle	7:00 p.m.
13	Dallas	7:00 p.m.
16	L.A. Clippers at Anaheim	7:30 p.m.
17	L.A. Lakers	7:00 p.m.
19	New York	5:00 p.m.
22	Orlando	4:30 p.m.
24	Charlotte	4:30 p.m.
25	Miami	4:30 p.m.
28	Minnesota	5:00 p.m.
30	Chicago	7:00 p.m.

D E C E M B E R

1	L.A. Lakers	7:30 p.m.
3	Milwaukee	2:00 p.m.
5	Phoenix	6:00 p.m.
7	Detroit	7:00 p.m.
10	Toronto	5:30 p.m.
13	Houston	7:00 p.m.
15	Portland	7:00 p.m.
16	Golden State	7:00 p.m.
18	Sacramento	7:30 p.m.
19	Seattle	7:00 p.m.
21	Seattle	7:00 p.m.
22	Phoenix	7:00 p.m.
26	Houston	5:30 p.m.
28	Dallas	5:30 p.m.
30	Boston	7:00 p.m.

J A N U A R Y

5	Philadelphia	7:00 p.m.
7	L.A. Clippers	2:00 p.m.
9	Golden State	7:30 p.m.
10	Denver	7:00 p.m.
12	Golden State	7:00 p.m.
13	Miami	7:00 p.m.
18	Cleveland	7:00 p.m.
20	New York	7:00 p.m.
22	Milwaukee	5:30 p.m.
24	Chicago	5:30 p.m.
25	Toronto	5:30 p.m.
27	Washington	4:30 p.m.
29	Philadelphia	4:30 p.m.
31	Boston	4:30 p.m.

F E B R U A R Y

2	New Jersey	7:00 p.m.
5	Utah	7:00 p.m.
7	Utah	6:00 p.m.
14	Sacramento	7:00 p.m.
16	Atlanta	7:00 p.m.
18	Seattle	12:30 p.m.
19	Phoenix	6:00 p.m.
25	San Antonio	12:30 p.m.
28	L.A. Lakers	7:00 p.m.

M A R C H

1	Dallas	7:00 p.m.
2	Denver	6:00 p.m.
4	Washington	7:00 p.m.
5	Golden State	7:30 p.m.
8	Indiana	7:00 p.m.
10	Houston	noon
11	Sacramento	7:30 p.m.
15	Orlando	7:00 p.m.
17	Minnesota	12:30 p.m.
19	New Jersey	4:30 p.m.
20	Atlanta	4:30 p.m.
22	Indiana	4:30 p.m.
24	Cleveland	10:00 a.m.
26	Detroit	4:30 p.m.
28	Denver	7:00 p.m.
29	Utah	6:00 p.m.
31	Charlotte	2:30 p.m.

A P R I L

2	Portland	7:00 p.m.
3	Minnesota	7:00 p.m.
5	L.A. Lakers	7:30 p.m.
7	Phoenix	noon
9	Houston	5:30 p.m.
10	San Antonio	5:30 p.m.
12	Sacramento	7:00 p.m.
14	Portland	noon
16	San Antonio	7:00 p.m.
18	Utah	7:00 p.m.
19	Denver	6:00 p.m.
21	L.A. Clippers	3:00 p.m.

All Times PST

■ Home games

■ Away games

a c k n o w l e d g e m e n t s

Opus Productions Inc.

President/Creative Director: Derik Murray

Vice President, Production: David Counsell

Design/Electronic Art: Guylaine Rondeau

Electronic Art: Paul Despins

Visual Coordinator: Joanne Powers

Design Consultant: Jeff McLean

Vice President/Publishing Director: Marthe Love

Chief Financial Officer: Jamie Engen

Legal Counsel: John Nicolls

Project/Editorial Coordinator: Wendy Darling

Editor: Brian Scrivener

Assistant Editorial Coordinator: Michelle Hunter

Marketing Manager: David Attard

Marketing Consultant: Glenn McPherson

Opus Productions would like to thank the management and staff of the Vancouver Grizzlies and Orca Bay Sports & Entertainment, especially the following:

Arthur Griffiths, Co-chairman, Chief Executive Officer and Governor

Stu Jackson, Executive Vice President of Basketball Operations and General Manager

Tom Mayenknecht, Vice President, Communications and Public Relations

Deborah Butt, Media Relations Coordinator

Noah Croom, Assistant General Manager and General Counsel

Tod Leiweke, Executive Vice President, Business

Steve Daniel, Basketball Information Coordinator

Steve Frost, Director of Media Relations

Kalli Quinn, Executive Assistant, Communications

Sharon Mey, Corporate Communications Coordinator

Melodi Kitagawa, Executive Assistant

Tammy Oliver, Executive Assistant

Trish Soper, Administrative Assistant

Opus Productions appreciates the generous assistance and support of the National Basketball Association, and extends special thanks to:

National Basketball Association Properties, Inc.

Frank Fochetta, Director and Group Manager, NBA Publishing

Diane Naughton, Director of Publishing

National Basketball Association Entertainment, Inc.

Carmin Romanelli, Manager, NBA Photos

Joe Amati, Photo Assistant

Eric Weinstein, Photo Assistant

National Basketball Association Communications Group

Alex Sachare, Vice President, Editorial

Mark Broussard, Staff Writer

Opus Productions is grateful to the following individuals and institutions for their assistance and support:

Dr. James Naismith Basketball Foundation
Almonte, Ontario
John Gosset

Naismith Memorial Basketball Hall of Fame
Springfield, Massachusetts
Wayne Patterson

Ken Allen, Evan Hargreaves, Nike Canada • Richard Belcher, Winning Spirit • Kate Bowden, Becky Lloyd-Scalco, Nike Inc. • Michael Burch, Nick Rundall, Whitecap Books Limited • Nancy Dodd, Rackets and Runners • Jerry Eberts • Robin Evans • Linda Goodman, Don Ogden, Supreme Graphics • Diane Grant • Mary Hermant • Steve McKinnon, City of Toronto Archives • Melinda Misener • David Schmidt, Spalding Canada • Allie Wilmink

---

Author's Note

There are several people without whose assistance this book would not have been possible. I would like to thank my wife Susan Walsh, whose patience, understanding and support were never ending and who made many sacrifices for which I am forever grateful. I would also like to thank Arthur Griffiths and Stu Jackson for their time and valuable insight into the process that resulted in the birth of the franchise and the building of the team.

Also deserving are my bosses and co-workers at The Canadian Press.

DOUG SMITH

Photo Credits

Baptist, Bill/NBA Photos: 108 2nd from bottom; **Bernstein, Andrew D.**/NBA Photos: 3, 32 left, 33, 34, 35 right, 36-37, 40 left, 41 bottom right, 45 left, 50, 51 bottom left, 54-55, 62 top left, 68-69, 71 right, 80 right, 83 right, 86 bottom, 99 bottom right, 100 right, 101 left, 108 3rd from bottom; **Bettmann/UPI**: 28, 29 left & right, 30 left & right, 31; **Butler, Nathaniel S.**/NBA Photos: 14 left & right, 17, 35 left, 39, 40 right, 44, 48 left, 53, 57 bottom, 59, 63 right, 66 left, 73 top right, 76, 78-79 top & bottom, 80 left, 81 top & bottom, 82 left & right, 83 top left, 84, 87, 88, 92 right, 93 left & bottom right, 95 right, 97 top & bottom, 99 top left, top right & bottom

left, 101 right, 103 top & bottom left, 105 left, 107, 109 top; **Capozzola, Lou**/NBA Photos: 77 left, 85; Courtesy of **City of Toronto Archives, Globe & Mail Collection**: 27 top #110886 & bottom #110884; **Cunningham, Scott**/NBA Photos: 41 bottom left, 46-47, 48 left, 56, 62 bottom left, 73 bottom left, 74 right, 75 right, 83 bottom left, 92 left, 108 bottom; **Defrisco, Tim**/Allsport: 52 right, 62 bottom right; **Defrisco, Tim**/NBA Photos: 58 left, 64 right; **Drake, Brian**/NBA Photos: 57 top; **Forencich, Sam**/NBA Photos: 71 left, 73 left; **Gossage, Barry**/NBA Photos: 45 right, 49, 66 top right, 67, 77 right, 109 3rd from bottom;

Grieshop, John F./ Schwartzman Sports: 109 2nd from bottom; **Hayt, Andy**/NBA Photos: 10, 62 top right, 63 left, 64 left, 70, 74 left, 86 top left & top right, 93 top right, 94, 95 top left, 98, 100 left, 104 left & top right, 105 right; **Hayt, Jon**/NBA Photos: 103 bottom right, 104 bottom right, 106 left & right; **Hoshino, Michio**/First Light: 102; **James, Glenn**/ NBA Photos: 72; Courtesy of **Kent Kallberg Studios**/Orca Bay: 4, 8, 9, 13 top & bottom, 15 right, 16 left & right; **Lovero, V. J.**/NBA Photos: 108 3rd from top; **McElligott, William**: 18, 22 left & right, 24-25; **McGrath, Frank**/ NBA Photos: 108 2nd from top; **Millan, Manny**/Sports Illustrated: 51

top, 58 right; **Murdoch, Layne**/NBA Photos: 66 bottom right; Courtesy of **Naismith Foundation, Almonte, Ont.**: 23; Courtesy of **Naismith Memorial Basketball Hall of Fame**: 19, 20 top & bottom, 21, 26; **Perdue, Norm**/NBA Photos: 109 3rd from top; Courtesy of **Relke, Chris J.**/Orca Bay: 15 left; **Schwartzman, Bruce L.**: 109 bottom; **Sierra, Hector**/NBA Photos: 52 left; **Soohoo, Jon**/NBA Photos: 32 right; **Stroud, Jason**/Derik Murray Photography Inc.: 6, 12, 38, 60-61, 89, 90; **Trotman, Noren**/NBA Photos: 41 top, 51 bottom right, 65, 109 2nd from top; **Vinnick, Jeff**/Vancouver Sun: 11; **Widner, Rocky**/NBA Photos: 75 left, 108 top.

Hoops comes home!
Get inside the action with this complete guide to basketball and the NBA.

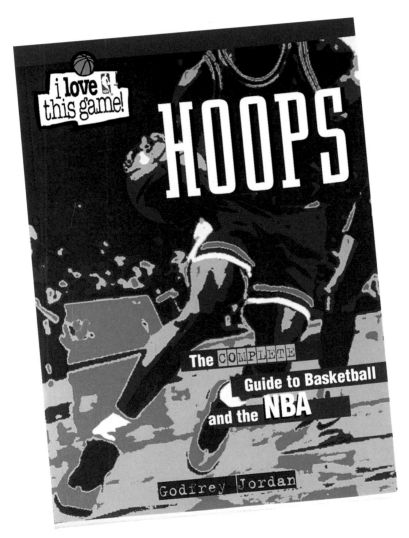

Since its creation in 1891 by a young Canadian, Dr. James Naismith, basketball has been a part of our national sports scene in schools and local leagues. Did you know the NBA's very first game was played at Maple Leaf Gardens in 1946 with the Toronto Huskies up against the New York Knicks!

Hoops! shows you the game's evolution, the basic rules, player positions, strategies and little-known highlights of hoop history. You'll learn how to translate the box scores and stay informed with a complete dictionary of basketball terms and a team directory.

Fully endorsed by the NBA, *Hoops!* is illustrated throughout and includes a colour photo section, charts and stats. A must for every fan – young and old – *Hoops!* is your fast break to follow all the action.

Now available in bookstores everywhere.